THE
LAST
SANDSTORM

by JASMIN FAULK-DICKERSON

A Memoir

ISBN: 978-1-66782-927-2 (softcover)
ISBN: 978-1-66782-928-9 (eBook)

To Zac, Dante, and Eros

The stars aligned just right for me and Daddy to meet,

our union was the prequel to the greatest manifestation of our love, you.

CONTENTS

FOREWORD

Jasmin Faulk-Dickerson has written a memoir that enriches her readers through a shared sense of human longing, ingenuity, and imagination. Stories like hers enjoin us to remember that the most astonishing things happen not in fiction, where they would be unbelievable, but in life stories. Jasmin's story provokes a powerful response, a desire to root for that bold and subtle girl with the indomitable spirit whose Italian/Saudi heritage opens her to the possibility of living more freely.

Jasmin's childhood in Riyadh is, at once, uplifting and ominous, traditional and unconventional, purposeful and perplexing. Her sense of internal contradiction grows as she measures her homelife in Saudi Arabia against summer vacations in her mother's country of origin, Italy, where she becomes immersed in pop culture and the undifferentiated socializing of western teens. Her imagination burgeons and she turns her sights from the middle east to the Magic Kingdom, where she visits and acquaints herself with a version, albeit fanciful, of American culture. Readers are reminded that music, theater, film, cartoons, and television can be more than entertainment. Jasmin's encounter with western culture becomes positively liberatory. I dare anyone to mock Mickey Mouse after reading Jasmin's story.

Yet Jasmin's freedom isn't merely an imaginative act or a tourist activity. From her earliest childhood memories through her marriage to a Saudi man, she stays focused on a life where she can become fully realized–not just a piece of property transferred from father to husband but a person with intrinsic power and agency. Needless to say, her escape from the Kingdom requires planning as much as a nascent belief in herself. Jasmin portrays the shocking reality of what it means to leave her mother and father, her siblings, all she holds dear–without the promise of a reunion. She understands what it means to live through her last sandstorm. Most of us can't imagine such a departure, and that is the gift of this book, which asks us to believe in the impossible.

—Sara Huntington
Member of the Faculty, Emerita
The Evergreen State College
The Last Sandstorm, Editor

PART ONE:

The Yearning

BETWEEN THE MIDDLE EAST AND WEST

Riyadh, Saudi Arabia—1980

I lay on the ground in the courtyard of our home. I stared for hours watching underneath the large gate that kept me enclosed behind the ten-foot concrete walls of my childhood home in the Kingdom's capital. My mom was not home. She was at a tea party with other western wives of Saudi men, where in the seventies and eighties, they gathered for social interludes at a different home each time, and where, I suspect, they talked about daily life as well as pressing taboo new-age topics in the conservatively Muslim community where they lived.

For a six-year-old, a couple of hours felt like an eternity, and no doubt I was already experiencing severe anxiety, even though I did not know it. I was confused; my mental and emotional realities conflicted with what was my cultural reality. I saw people leave the house daily for different reasons, but as a little girl, my place was at school or at home, and on occasion with my mother at social gatherings. Lying on the ground, I worried my Italian mom would not come back; *what if she were in a car accident? What if someone kidnapped her? What if she decided to leave us?* These feelings were in misalignment with my family's belief system but echoed the disconnect from my Saudi culture and amplified my sense of unworthiness and paranoia.

My father took my older brother Yasser with him to work every day, where he learned the business world at our dad's furniture showroom store and where my brother watched men interact in formal social ways. This exposure, that only males were entitled to, and one that profoundly influenced Yasser, aided in his successful future as a journalist, media personality and social figure, both in the Middle East and in the West.

By contrast, my younger sister, May, and I lamented as we watched Yasser dressed in formal clothes and doused with cologne, take off with our father while we spent the afternoons and evenings at home with our Filipina nanny, Ella. Ella was special, and more like an aunt than a nanny. She humored us and played with us, but we yearned for a more social and normal life with boys and girls our age. At the office, Yasser was surrounded by men of various cultures and ages, enriched by an exposure that he admits he did not fully appreciate at the time. By contrast May and I were surrounded by walls, domesticated, enriched by video cassettes in our Betamax player that patronized us, showing us samples of a liberated world and the enticing American teen life.

During that time, I began to realize I was entertaining some controversial thoughts and did not feel at peace with my young and peculiar life. I started to experience intense fear and disturbing worry. It wasn't until years later, and after much therapy, that I began to understand the root of my anxiety; my childhood felt like juggling torches while standing on a tightrope, totally untrained but amusing to others. As a child I had few words to articulate the innate and instinctual fear of losing the stability and security of my mom and dad's wholeness. In my world nothing seemed to offer unquestionable stability because my family was a hybridized transplant. To this I responded with profound and intuitive fear as it manifested in internal anxiety and proud stoicism, even as a young girl.

On Fridays, the holy day of rest for Muslims, we donned our pretty clothes and my father drove us in his golden Mercedes to family and friends, where we visited over a cup of tea and sweets. As we dressed and readied ourselves to leave the house, my dad stood in the main hallway, in front of the mirror in partial light, chewing mint gum and adjusting his headdress, sometimes humming, other times quiet. I often asked him for a piece of gum. I didn't always get it, but when I did, I assessed his mood as optimal and playful, and felt excited about the day. It was one of the few ways I connected with my introverted father.

I was in second grade before I realized that my father was not the King of Saudi Arabia. Like the founder of the Kingdom, my father's name was Abdulaziz, "Servant of God," in Arabic. I often wondered why everyone talked about my father, King Abdulaziz. I saw pictures of the royal men, all dressed in traditional Saudi clothing, like my father, all sporting a mustache, like my father, and all of them looking quite regal, like my father.

LOGIC DOES NOT EXIST

October 10th, 2018.

I began the fall quarter of graduate school and sat in class consumed by the thoughts of my ill father far away. After seven weeks in the hospital, the news I dreaded to hear arrived. My brother called to tell me that our father had passed away. The last year or so of his life, his body endured the many challenging consequences of a lifetime of little self-care and poor habits. In childhood, I learned how to measure his level of stress through his moods and degree of consumption, whether it was smoking a pack a day or drinking beverages I was not allowed to taste. My father was an artist, troubled by the creative force within him, and by the confines of his culture, which amputated the limbs of his passion and intellect. The last time I saw my father was in 1999. When he died, the last thread of attachment to a country that gave me little to hold on to, was cut. But with his passing, I began to re-evaluate everything about his identity and mine. I became preoccupied with developing an understanding of who my father was, beyond who I thought he was.

Born in the very young, and recently founded Kingdom of Saudi Arabia, my father grew up in the northern part of the country, the city of Hail, in a mud house built by his father and older brothers. Later on, he recalled being old enough to participate in the expansion of the house and used his hands to build walls and rooms of mud. His childhood home was a striking slice of Arabian history and of tribal progress. When I visited New Mexico for the first time I was stunned by the uncanny similarities between the adobe homes in this Southwestern state and my father's hometown in a desert thousands of miles away. When my father died, the only other place that seemed fitting to celebrate his life was, in fact, Albuquerque, even though he had never set foot in the United States.

My siblings and I reunited privately and quietly in remembrance of our father. We rented an adobe home within walking distance of the old town Albuquerque, and when we were not going through photographs of our father, or recalling childhood memories, we were walking through the streets and alleys of this town that made us feel closer to our father than we, perhaps, ever did during his life on his land.

My father was educated by intellectuals and teachers in meetings that were nothing like schools today. He spent a few hours daily learning from these masters how to read and write, and soon he was nominated for an upgraded program for gifted students, where he would study to become a teacher of the upcoming batch of eager Saudi boys. His teachers realized he had the X factor, and, after observing him in the classroom for a few years, the Saudi government chose him as one of a handful of students to be sent abroad on a full scholarship where he would be trained and educated, eventually becoming part of the first generation of Saudi professionals. He was the youngest, but also the first and only in his immediate family—conservative and humble—to obtain a full education. My father was somewhat of a wallflower, and I knew very little of his childhood and life. I learned about him in bits and pieces, either through accidental comments he dropped that revealed some of these details or through what my brother would report he learned from the elders.

My father's mother, Nura, birthed him in the late 1930's; she survived the birth, when many women didn't, but her health was frail, and she was unable to breastfeed him. His older brother, presumed to be about twenty-five years his senior (birth certificates did not exist in those days, and we do not have exact documentation of births and deaths from back then), was married. His wife, Alya, had just delivered her second child, and without hesitation took on the role of nursing my father, her brother-in-law, as well. This was a story my father told in a short sentence, "I owe everything to ummi Alya," (*ummi* my mother, in Arabic). His own mother, my grandmother—whom I never met—passed away when my father was in his mid-twenties. I sensed a deep sadness when he occasionally mentioned her, but his loss was soothed by the presence of the other mother in his life, who, after all, was the woman who fed him when he was an infant and gave him hope for survival during a time when many infants died of malnutrition and disease, including some of his own siblings. "Don't forget to kiss her head," he would remind me of the way elders are greeted, a gesture that he never failed to display with Alya. I wanted to view her as the paternal grandmother I never had, but an unexplainable resistance on her part made it clear I was to address her as my uncle's wife.

I asked my father questions about his childhood: His response came in the form of a partial shy smile, eyes lost in thought, and I was left to create a biography of the man I idolized but knew so little about. How did a traditional Saudi boy go from living in a small premodern town, to becoming the man I knew growing up: educated, multi-lingual, stylish, and worldly. My father was a puzzle of many small pieces that sat mixed in a box. At every pivotal moment in my life, I attempted to piece together some of those odd shapes in order to understand him and feel closer to him. No matter how hard I tried to assemble the whole picture, I had to settle with fragments of the mystery that was my father.

He was a kind-hearted man; dare I say innocent and naive in many ways. His heart was pure, and his intentions were always good. He was mild tempered and soft spoken. In fact, these observations stem from the fact that I don't recall ever seeing my father angry when I was a young child. He was instinctively affectionate. Hugs and kisses came to him naturally, and he displayed similar genuine affections towards animals. It would seem as though he was the perfect man and perfect father, and while in many ways he was, there were certain crucial elements that were missing. The culture he grew up in and the family he was part of taught him to be reserved and highly concerned with the opinion and approval of others. This was a huge struggle for me later on in adolescence, when I began to have ideas and ambitions, only to be dismissed by my father's strong sense of societal responsibility and cultural obligations. When I was a preteen, I asked him if I could take horseback riding lessons, and without making eye contact, he said, simply, "Those activities are for people that want to show off, and that is not who we are."

Who were we? Identity seemed to be a character that never changed its costume, no matter how many different scenes or plays it appeared in. Everything revolved around one's identity, and yet, there was no room for developing it. There was a default standard by which one could measure and present their identity, achieved by conforming to social practices, dress-code, and self-imposed boundaries. This was my life in Saudi Arabia.

My father was the only member of our family with a native identity. As a child, I created in my mind, based on reality and imagination, many identities of my father: Papà, king, architect, teacher, businessman, brother, husband, boss, employer, son-in-law, Saudi, Italian…and priest. When he traveled outside of Saudi Arabia because work sent him around Europe or when vacation called for him to visit the Italian in-laws, my father wore western clothes, usually a suit, but on occasion casual slacks and a buttoned-up shirt. In Saudi Arabia, at home, he wore a "thobe," the traditional long dress men wear. Outside the home, he wore a thobe, and a "ghutra," the white headdress many Arab men, in the Arabian Peninsula, wear. Now and then, while on vacation in Italy, he would wear a thobe indoors, for comfort. One summer, while staying on the beach of Jesolo, not far from Venice, in Italy, my father stepped out on the balcony of our nineth floor condo in his thobe; within minutes, a crowd below gathered and stared at this mysteriously mystic priest-like figure. My father, not at all a social clown, surprised me with his response to the comical attention he was receiving. He raised his arms in the air as if offering benediction to all who watched. I was a very amused nine-year-old.

In fourth grade, when I started writing with ink, I was proud to use a pen which had my father's business name printed on it. It was a maroon pen with blue ink. My father was the founder and general manager of his architecture and furniture store. His relationship with Italy began when he was a student and continued when he became a businessman. He traveled several times a year with his rich Saudi clients, some of whom were members of the royal family, to select the latest furniture designs from the exhibits in Milan, as well as other European cities like Zurich, Geneva, Paris, and Frankfurt. Some of his clients had children who were friends of mine at school, and I beamed with pride when I saw them writing with pens advertising my dad's business. My father was a rock star! I felt especially important when I would—almost daily—call him at work to ask him random questions. It was an excuse to say, "Can I speak to Abdulaziz?" when the operator answered the phone. My father was very patient, and with his sweet murmurous voice he would say, "Wait till I get home," after I would insist, "Can I take some gum from your room?" I didn't care about the gum as much as I cared to have his attention. I wanted the person answering the phone to know I was his daughter. I felt excited when they would ask, "Who's calling?" because it meant that I got to brag about being Abdulaziz's daughter, but also because I was conducting business like an adult.

In the early 1960's when Saudi Arabia sent its first group of Saudi Students to study abroad, selections were made based on careers, professions of interest and countries of destination: Medical students were sent to India and Pakistan, technology students to the United States, and engineering students to Europe. My father was interested in architecture and design, and was sent to the Academy of Fine Arts, in Florence, Italy. Before they set off for their schools, the Saudi boys were sent to either Egypt or Lebanon—two of the most modern Arab countries—where they were acclimated to "the real world," countries where they would see unveiled women, cars, modern buildings, and encounter unfamiliar social situations and 20th century inventions for the first time.

In the early months of their education, they were placed in host families to learn the language. In an uncharacteristic display, my father would recount, "We worked so hard to learn the basic Italian words in the first few days. Mohammad was committed to making a good impression the first morning with his host family. He sat at the breakfast table and exclaimed, "*Banjara!*" This story always made me laugh hard, especially because of the way my father delivered it. His unusual, animated side showed up once in a blue moon, and stories like these were the perfect platform. *Banjara*—which sounded like a very Saudi word—was my father's friend Mohammad's attempt at saying *Buongiorno*. My father learned the Italian language in a short time and remained fluent his whole life. Growing up we spoke Italian at home, and up until the last time I spoke with him a few weeks before his passing, my father and I communicated in Italian.

Conversations with my father were ninety-five percent in Italian with some occasional Arabic, but conversations with my father were also brief and superficial. When I brought home my monthly report card from school, he would put on his reading glasses and go straight to my grades in math and science. He praised my achievements in one word, "Good," then glanced over to the rest of the subjects, most of them Islamic studies, which I passed with a dull and unmotivated C. He assured me, "I care less about your accomplishments in these subjects, as long as you pass them." I felt validated by him and didn't need him to say much more about that. School was not a priority for me, and while education was important to him, I knew he trusted my private school teaching and celebrated my standardized and modest academic success.

I came to realize that my father could only be known through observation. Words were not his thing. I had to let go of that desperate longing to anchor my relationship with him through language. One early morning, when I was in the throes of adolescence, I was struck by a need for him in ways he could not comprehend. He sat alone, quietly, in the family room, perhaps still awake from the night before, preoccupied with thoughts that I was never privy to. I yearned so desperately to talk to him about my dreams, my worries, and wanted to hear a motivational lecture from him, one that he drew from his own life and experiences, one that would give me some insight into who he was deep inside, and how he faced the obstacles of life—which for him had been many. I wanted to see myself in him and see the young and ambitious him in me. I longed for a conversation about the confines and boundaries of my personal freedom—my future.

Few words ever came out of his mouth, and many of those words made little sense to me, because I wanted more from him. Rather than soliciting a profoundly intellectual discussion—which I knew was impossible—I settled for the default parent-teen dialogue, starting out with, "Can I do…?" or "Can I have…?" This was when I asked him if I could join the equestrian club, one of the few extracurricular activities which were offered to girls. The idea of bonding with a horse and learning horseback riding—with my best friend Reem, who did it weekly— symbolized a sense of freedom and empowerment. I knew the answer without asking the question; it wasn't telepathy, but I could read my father's mind just by looking at his eyes and his mouth. His soft and intimidated gaze reflected the vulnerability he had developed as the youngest of seven, and solidified by cultural demands. His lips pursed and his eyes blinked slowly. Many of my questions and requests were halted with responses like "That's not who we are," and a simple, "No." Even though most of his rejections hurt, I would have accepted them more gracefully if he had offered a heartfelt explanation to go along with the dismissal.

But all I got was his unfathomable one-liners. I desperately sighed and said "Papà, that's just not logical!" With a slight delay and measured deliberation, he terminated our brief interaction—interminable by his standards— he softly, but firmly said, "Logic does not exist."

A BOOK TO RE-READ

It didn't rain often in Saudi Arabia, and I remember how frequently the King organized *Istisqua*, rain prayers in the holy mosques. Praying for rain was a desperate plea for sustaining many hardy lifeforms in the harsh deserts of the Arabian Peninsula. When it rained, everyone was happy, but I felt depressed. It wasn't until I was much older that I realized that my earliest memory of rain coincided with the day I watched *Bambi* for the first time.

I was still in kindergarten, too young to understand death, but old enough to fear loss. My mom, who knew how much I loved animals and who often referred to me as "Angelo Lombardi, amico degli animali," a famous Italian personality and host of a TV show about animals, enjoyed watching me sing all the songs from the *Jungle Book* in Italian. My fascination with the story had much to do with my envy of Mowgli's life with animals. On a weekend afternoon in December, after playing outside in our courtyard, still wearing my shiny blue jacket and thick brown socks with my green bellbottom corduroy pants—an outfit I loved to wear when I was not in my school uniform—I plopped in front of the TV where my mom was waiting to play another Disney movie featuring animated creatures. She believed *Bambi* would satisfy the animal and Disney lover in me. I never had the heart to tell her she was wrong and that, in fact, *Bambi* was the first tool that allowed me to identify *la mia croce fissa*, my cross to bear.

At my age, loss only meant one thing, not having my mother, and *Bambi* proved that even younglings could lose their mother. I didn't want to see my mother in characters who suffered, like Bambi's mother and Mrs. Jumbo, Dumbo's mother. More to my taste was *The Sound of Music*, where I saw the elegant and beautiful Baroness Schrader, known to Captain von Trapp simply as Elsa, who unlike Bambi's mother and Mrs. Jumbo, shared my mother's elegance, vivaciousness, and name.

Born at the end of WWII, my Elsa was the daughter of Southern Italian teachers, who, after her birth in a small village in the province of Potenza, south of Naples, set their ambitions towards a more intellectually and culturally rich life for their two daughters in the Tuscan capital, and world center of renaissance accomplishments, Florence.

My maternal grandmother, Nonna Teresa, whose family origins were aristocratic and noble, was a gentle and kind woman. She was educated during a time when only few women in elite families received an education. Instead of taking her privilege for granted, she became a teacher in the village where she grew up. She was a devout catholic but also a feminist at heart, as she postponed marriage to establish herself and career.

Her husband, my grandfather, Nonno Franco, whose family appeared to be hardworking simple folk, was also of noble origins, although his family's status was diluted and then forgotten because of how many members had immigrated. Beyond my maternal cousins in Italy, I have cousins in the UK, South America, and North America. Nonno Franco was a stoic and masculine figure. Unlike his devout wife, he was an atheist and as the oldest of seven children, including two sisters who became nuns, his parents' aspiration to see him fulfill a life in priesthood was boldly halted when he chose the path of dedicated husband, exemplary father, and committed teacher. In his early adulthood he traveled to Northern Africa with the Italian military, where he had his first encounter with the Arab culture and way of life. He never spoke to me about this time, but I spent hours during quiet afternoons in my grandparents' home, sitting in silence next to my grandfather, witnessing the encounters he had in the capital of Libya, Tripoli, through his camera lens in an album he documented with handwritten notes. One photo that he captioned "Beautiful Bedouin Girl," made me wonder if in his own granddaughter he saw that young woman again.

My mother's childhood sounded like a fable: her trips to the vegetable market with her mother to select produce for dinner, baking mud pies in the courtyard of their home using bottle caps as decorations and playing with curtain tassels as wigs in defiance of her father's inexplicable ban on bangs. She idolized her sister, who was ten years her senior and suffered greatly in her teens when my aunt, Zia Flora, married and left Florence, heading north with her husband. My mother was an open book, and she talked about her childhood casually, sharing anecdotes in which I detected a strain of melancholy.

My mom joined my sister and me in the family room, after her *riposo* every afternoon. One of our pastimes following homework and while we waited for dinner was watching TV shows and pausing often to talk. Many incidents in the western shows we watched paralleled her life and she would remember special movie dates with her older sister, going to the farmer's market, running errands, playing with neighborhood friends, visiting the library, and riding the bus. The part that she didn't realize back then was that her life could not have been more different than the life I was living as a child. I look back now and am so thankful she was oblivious to this, because had she realized it, she might have filtered her stories and measured herself. I admit that during my adolescence I resented the comparison between her life and mine. She often emphasized how strict my grandfather was and how her curfew of 7 p.m. was the harshest among her friends. I argued that a life confined to the walls of my home was far worse. I didn't know what a movie theater was, I couldn't play with the neighborhood kids whom I had never met, riding a bus seemed like an amusement park adventure, and...what was a library?

My mom's gift of storytelling was perhaps due to the fact that she was, and still is, an avid reader. Her stories have stayed with me, like the one of her middle school friend, Stafania Salemi, who once asked her, "Why are you so fat?" not at all concerned with the fact that she was inches shorter than my mom and twice as heavy. This offhand comment nevertheless prompted my mother to go on a diet, forever maintaining a slender and elegant figure.

I also loved her descriptions of her favorite books. I could almost picture the one with the red cover, or the one that she read over and over, the series that she collected weekly, and the classics that she asked for as birthday presents. She introduced us to *Little Women* and *Pinocchio* before I could read Italian. I learned of all the classics of literature from an Italian perspective, like Hans Christian Anderson's *Little Mermaid*, and Stevenson's *Treasure Island*. Books were her most valued possession, and during the tragic 1966 flood of the Arno River in Florence, which killed over 100 people and destroyed millions of historic masterpieces, she was devastated at having to choose between joining the "Mud Angels"—the endearing name given to the many students who volunteered to save, dry and preserve these Italian treasures—and helping her family by traveling north with her older sister, making it possible for her parents and grandparents, who lived in the same home, to survive the limited water supply in the city during that time. She confessed, "It was a tough decision, I wanted to save the books in the library I spent so many hours in," but she didn't hesitate and chose her family, a revelation that influenced my own struggle between what I wanted and what I had to do.

Growing up in the cultural capital of the world was a privilege my mom never took for granted. She was well informed about the history of Europe, and an expert in Italian timeline achievements. I didn't know what a home-schooled education was at the time, but my mother homeschooled us in a natural and casual way. Everything I learned from her far exceeded the knowledge I brought home from school. "Dante Alighieri described the state of limbo in his section dedicated to the purgatory, an example of how we struggle in life between states of change," she would say before reciting parts of the Divine Comedy by heart, often moved to tears by such masterpieces. In her youth she spent summers in her birth village where she was reminded of humility and community, a quality her parents strongly instilled in her as a way to remain grounded in the midst of their sophisticated and entitled life in Florence.

She was interested in languages and regretted never learning German, but since her dream career was to become an interpreter and journalist, she decided instead to major in French and English and spent a year in the UK as well as a month in France during her college studies.

My love for Scotland was ignited in my youth when my mother shared stories and pictures of her time visiting the many beautiful parts of the United Kingdom with her host family, the Stathams. One of my favorite pictures is a snapshot of her with their deaf Dalmatian dog, Snookie, in their lush garden in Darby. My mother spoke fondly of her time in England, "The Stathams welcomed me like family. It was so natural for me to be with them since they had hosted your Zia before me," a sentiment she expressed whenever we talked about her time in England. She also reminisced about her visits with Joan and "Bruttino" (a nickname given lovingly to Joan's husband Godfrey, by my Zia, the Italian word for "a little ugly") who for no reason except goodwill had become dear family friends after the first encounter with my Zia on a bus. These stories were encouraging because they highlighted the best of humanity and affirmed the power of kindness. It is perhaps because of this notion, I, like my mother and her family, have invested in beautiful —sometimes distant— and long-lasting friendships.

"My time in England was life changing," she said casually in the face of the changes that continued in her life and of which I was a part. In her year in England, she made many friends, and spent time with her uncle Nicola, his wife Gerarda, and her first cousins who were raised in England. My great uncle Nicola, who fought in the Italian military during WWII, was a Prisoner of War (POW), held by the British in India. By the end of the war, he was transferred to England with many other POWs and held in British prisons until the end of the war when all soldiers were released and given the option to return to their country of origin or remain in the UK and gain citizenship. Instead of returning to a devastated post-fascism Italy amid financial and war ruin, my uncle stayed and established a life for himself, bringing his family to England and starting a successful Gelato company. My mom's first impression of driving in England was when she rode in their ice-cream truck. She noted, "I got my driver's license in Italy but never drove; I understood the rules of driving, but I was horrified at the sight of cars coming towards us on what appeared to be the wrong side of the road!" I listened to her describe this event without asking many questions, I just let my mind play the movie, starring my mom. On that ride, her cousin Antonio blasted the radio and the music playing caught my mom's attention, "Who is this?" She asked Antonio.

"WHAT?! You don't know who this is?" He asked in shock.

"No, I haven't heard this before," she admitted.

"You don't know *The Beatles*?!" He exclaimed.

My mom bragged about how she got to hear "Twist and Shout" months before The Beatles invaded all of Europe. She would tell us, "Picture it being Duran Duran before you heard of them!" Decades later, she still recalls how that was the first Beatles record she ever bought.

Life in Italy and England must have been wonderful, I thought. *How did she then choose to leave that all behind and move to the Middle East? To Saudi Arabia?* I asked her that many times, eventually just rhetorically because I learned that she didn't have an answer. I never stopped wondering how she could have left that all behind. Her responses were always vague and unconvincing, "This is our home; this is our country. I would do it all over again if I had to." She was uncomfortable with my questioning her, and yet her storytelling on occasion revealed her longing. I wanted to believe that she was sure of the choices she made, and as I got older, I accepted that she was able to love and cherish both countries she called home, but I was in denial about the suggestion that in Saudi Arabia she found equal gratification to the freedoms offered in Europe.

My mother described how strict my grandfather was, and how he was not shy of making it clear that not many young men were worthy of Elsa. She was his little girl. "Zia Flora *is* happy in Italy because she has the simple life she wanted," my mother parroted her father's opinion about her sister, who everyone believed was more like their mother and who would be content with a traditional life and family. Flora was religious, domestic, and dutiful. Accordingly, she married her childhood sweetheart, and became a teacher. She had two sons and lived a picture-perfect modest Italian life, which included her live-in parents-in-law.

On the other hand, when my mom spoke to me about her hunger for knowing other cultures, and her fascination with history, I understood that she sought inner growth and intellectual expansion. She bashfully shared with me and my sister how young men of all walks of life tried to court her. Her silent crushes on the good-looking blond German boy, or the mystery guy on the bus, innocently kept her blushing; then there was the Indian prince who tried to charm her, to no avail. She didn't seem distracted by the pursuit of a husband. She was a post-war modern woman, a thinker, a talented orator, and a gifted writer. Reading and writing were her passions and, later on in life, she published over a dozen books in Italian in the personal growth and self-help genre. Growing up I didn't realize that she was a renaissance woman. I was distracted by her persona as mother, wife, and teacher, roles in which she naturally also drew, painted, cooked, sewed, crocheted, created arts and crafts, did pyrography, etched glass, and hosted elegant tea parties. She kept busy, and perhaps that's the one thing I have learned from her. Staying busy can be a distraction, other times therapy, but usually it is just a way of being.

As I continued to seek my own identity through every milestone I faced and wall I ran into, I strove to understand both my parents, which I knew was the only way I could get closer to my own truth. How did these two vastly different individuals end up together? Was their union the root of all my struggles and torment?

I visualized what my mom described as that first encounter between her and my father like a scene from a romantic movie. Her life capsized one Christmas during her college years, when she attended a student party—without the official consent of her father—a party she was dragged to by a friend who had a crush on a young Arab man. Along with her friend's crush another handsome young man entered the room. It never dawned on my mother that he was not Italian, as his complexion and features were mirrors of young southern Italian boys, but he too was an Arab student attending the party as a fresh foreign newcomer. She insisted that when she saw him that very moment, she knew he was the man she was going to marry.

Theirs was love at first sight. In the early months of their courtship, my grandparents were not aware of this unfolding. My aunt and her husband were admitted to the secret romance when they arranged to take the young couple to Torre Del Lago for an outing. During that infamous day trip, my cousin, Vince, who at the time was a toddler, was told repeatedly not to mention meeting "Aziz" to his grandparents.

When my mom was dropped off at home by her sister, brother-in-law and nephew, my grandparents asked, "How was the outing?"

"Lovely," the three adults replied casually.

"Aziz was also there!" exclaimed the toddler, who could not contain himself.

My parents' six-year courtship experienced many ups and downs. My father had gone through the heartbreaking loss of his mother, who died in his arms only months before he left for Italy, a story I learned from my brother Yasser, and never heard told by my introverted father. His mother had been proud and worried about the fact that her son was embarking on a big and prestigious academic adventure. She was traditional and uneducated and couldn't imagine what awaited her youngest child in a faraway land where infidels and non-Arabs lived. She begged his best friend, who was also going to Italy as a student, to promise not to let her son bring back an *aj'nabiya*, a "foreign" woman. Breaking this promise, both my dad's best friend Sa'ad and my father married Tuscan women, and remained married to them a lifetime.

My mother, who was growing uncertain of her future with a foreign man, with foreign habits, living in a foreign land, broke it off at one point. She shared this tidbit with humor but without much thought. For me, this was a revelation. I understood why her denial was so strong when I questioned her life choices. At the time I was consumed with what was missing in my own life. I projected. I couldn't understand why she would give up all the things I wished for myself. In recounting her courtship, she admitted to us that the cultural differences were becoming clear, and her infatuation with this mysterious man was subsiding. He never gave up; he pursued her, charmed her, and won her back. Despite how lopsided their love became over the years, she declared that she always cared for our father, and that bringing her children into the world with him was the divine purpose behind all her choices, choices she never regretted.

I believe that it was more than that. Her adventurous spirit navigated its way towards a mysterious land where I observed her meeting inspirational and influential mentors. When she was growing up in Italy she engaged in the most intellectually profound teachings; in Saudi Arabia however, her mentors introduced her to the mystical realm of spirituality, where she sought a deeper meaning in life and a greater sense of self. As she grew spiritually, she confronted the limits of her marriage which focused on parental instead of existential goals. That didn't stop them from being lifelong partners. They both cared for one another, but most importantly, loved their children and, in their own way, expressed it.

Although my father remained a mystery my whole life, my mother, much like her greatest passion, was an intriguing book I love to read and reread.

DESERT SPROUT

I was born in 1974, when my parents had been married for five years and had recently moved into their first home, built brand new in a developing part of Riyadh. Our house was like an art gallery: Paintings by both my parents and other artists, as well as replica statues of famous Italian sculptures were in every room. My brother Yasser and I loved playing with a mini–Michelangelo's David that we took turns holding and carrying around. I would envision myself sucked into a colorful masterpiece of cubism art painted by my father, depicting an Arab village, that hung on the living room wall over the elaborate wallpaper. Why didn't all the homes have art on the walls? Why didn't they have a naked David displayed in the living room, and why did my parents later remove our David? This was an unusual childhood, an unusual home with unusual things. My infrequent visits to my Saudi relatives' homes and the few traditional Saudi families we knew brought me face to face with a world no one had explained to me. For years, the lack of couches and chairs in my uncles' houses made me think that they had not finished furnishing their homes. They didn't have bed frames, just layers of traditional, colorful, stuffed quilts as mattresses covering the entire floor of the bedroom that they called *Guss'r*, palace. As the years went by, they didn't seem to add any other furniture; who was odd, I wondered, us or them?

One of my earliest memories is a dream that took place in the house of another Saudi-Italian family that we knew, a house that felt familiar because they had art on the walls and chairs to sit on. In the dream, however, the house lacked furniture. My brother, sister, mom, and I sat quietly in their dark, unusually cold living-room. A large, monstruous woman entered the room and snatched my mom, threw her over her shoulder, and headed out the door. I can still feel the anger, pain, and panic of the dream. My siblings and I attacked the woman, jumped on her back, pulled our mom down, bit the monster's huge ankles and screamed like terrified pups.

When I woke up, I had tears coming down my face. I was breathless and scared. I was only four years old. Too young to understand my dream, or even verbalize it, I started to internalize my traumatized feelings and worries. I lived in constant fear that mom would go away or be taken from me. Today I look back at that dream and wonder if the mom-snatcher was my depiction of the culture I feared and didn't trust, even as a four-year-old.

It is perhaps a common worry that many children have at a young age, but mine was based in an uncommon reality. I had a sense that my mother did not belong in the same way most other women in my country did. When she spoke Arabic, she sounded different because she could not pronounce the throat-clearing letter, "*Kh.*" We spoke Italian at home, and I had to think about which words from which language to use when I was with others outside my home. We had a close circle of friends that were bi-cultural like us, and we socialized in a non-gender-segregated setting. Our house smelled like espresso and basil tomato sauce, instead of cumin and incense; it was furnished with classical Italian craftsmanship pieces and not layers of upholstered floor foam; and the rhythm of our family's punctual meals, bedtime, and daily routine was in stark contrast with the *bukra-inshallah*—tomorrow God willing—flow of the locals. My parents never made big mention of our cultural divergence, a silence that increased my sense of misplacement. Those were simple yet obvious influences that burdened me as a precocious and observant child.

I was alert and intuitive which made matters worse for a reserved child. My sense of empathy was debilitating, often causing my family to keep sad events and news from me. This sheltered me at times and spared me the immediate suffering, but ultimately it crippled my sense of coping and my ability to face trauma in my early adulthood. The uncertainty of my mom's belonging in the culture produced this taxing sense of fear, even though it was the farthest thing from my parents' mind, an unfounded notion to them since my mom had converted to Islam and become a Saudi citizen. She was an English teacher at the most prominent private school, where many of the royal children went, and where my siblings and I also attended for 12 years, from the first day of first grade to our high school graduation.

I was lucky to have a sister I was very close to. May and I are eighteen months apart and, although we are polar opposites, we have always been close. She was the beautiful, soft spoken, socially shy child, with the stormy Italian temper at home when provoked. I was the creative, strong willed, assertive leader, with a fragile, deeply sensitive, and worried mind. We were the yin to the other's yang. We had an unspoken understanding that made us relate like twins.

As young Arab girls, we were isolated from society. Outside of school we had a strictly limited social life. In our despair and loneliness, we put our creativity to work. We brought to life a world full of kings and queens, witches and wizards, best friends who were boys, not just girls, and fantasy creatures that would put to shame today's Hollywood CGI. We felt like outsiders in our own country more often than not and in Italy when we visited every summer, our time was too short to plant roots. Thus "Banga" was manifested from our very own imaginations, and it had become our country of choice, where "Kaninaise" (rhymes with mayonnaise) was our invisible best friend and with whom we spoke an invented language. In fact, our weekends became the world we lived in more fully. Packing a backpack and putting foil on my teeth to pretend I had braces like the kids in American movies, I headed to the backyard with May, still in the confinement of the ten-foot walls of our home, where we played in the small empty alley that to us was filled with thick forest trees, knights on horses, damsels in distress, and battles that could only be won by these two tough warriors and their best friend, Kaninaise!

As the hot sun took on the role of a blazing fire, I raced with Kaninaise into the forest because the queen was held against her will by the evil witch. On our way to the castle, we met the king who begged desperately, "Please! Go save the Queen! The wizards have tried and failed!" May was helping the village people escape and find shelter before she too joined us in the castle.

Hours would pass before we would successfully defeat the witch and leave her to melt under the sudden rainstorm; the four of us wounded but strong rode out of the castle on the back of a magical unnamed dragon. The story never changed, but the adventure was new every time. This was our escape.

It was during that time, in the late 1970's that I met a girl who soon became part of our family. At one of the many mom-kid tea parties we attended in our multi-cultural community, a new face emerged from behind a fort of sheets and pillows in the living-room. We were introduced by our mothers, who had only recently met through another mutual friend.

Cybèle was the adopted only-child of Berenice, a white Canadian professor at the University of King Saud for girls in Riyadh. Berenice was a product of the 1960s civil rights movement. She joined Dr. Martin Luther King, Jr.'s marches and embodied the true spirit of the era's activism. She was a feminist and trailblazer adopting a Black child as a single mother. When Berenice was handed her new baby girl, she was taken aback and thought it was a mistake because the infant was not Black. Turns out, the baby was not Black enough for Berenice. Cybèle, the biological child of a young Irish woman and a Jamaican father, was a light-skinned baby. These were all details I learned much later: At the time I had no concept of race and skin color, and I saw no distinction between the way Cybèle and I looked. "I'm white, and I'm Black," Cybèle would share. I listened without saying much, simply wondering why she didn't have a father.

It didn't take long for our mothers to become soul sisters, seeking and growing together in the captivating and emerging world of new age and positive thinking. Cybèle, also as a founding member of Banga, instantly gained three siblings as Yasser, May, and I started fighting for her attention and sworn BFF status. Closer in age, Cybèle and Yasser spent a lot of time together. During our family desert picnics, the two of them would go off on hikes leaving me and May behind, resentful. In the backyard under a secret tree, they hid crystal treasures salvaged from old chandeliers. I knew I was in the big kids' club when I too was given my first teardrop-shaped crystal, an initiation that told me I was important. But that changed one summer when Cybèle came back from boarding school. She and Yasser were clearly in the agonies of adolescent transformation. In response, my brother created a wedge between himself and the informality of his previous relationships, perhaps as a way to protect himself as a young man maturing in Saudi society.

On the contrary, Cybèle grew closer to me and May, and we spent days on end listening to cassettes, watching music videos, talking about boys, playing card games, board games, and visiting Banga. We were unapologetic pranksters. While playing hide-and-seek one time, I hid (fully clothed) in the swimming pool, watching both May and Cybèle pass me by unable to find me. I held my breath for close to a minute until I emerged spouting water from the blowhole on my face, evoking their disapproval. Every few months May and I would rearrange the posters on our walls or add new ones that Cybèle brought back from her travels for us.

Giggling, Cybèle and I asked May, "How do you like it?" after we redecorated her side of the wall.

"Why are you laughing?" May would ask frustrated and pouty.

"Nothing!" we would say as we stared at the poster that we had hung upside-down, and which took May weeks to notice.

When Cybèle was not at the house, we talked on the phone for hours. A seed was planted the day Yasser grew up: The collective garden of our childhood bonds on Saudi soil took root. With him out of the picture, the girls' friendship germinated and survived vast geographical displacements. I rejoiced in receiving Garfield postcards from England. Cybèle's notes invited me to experience her boarding school life with friends and horses, which filled me with delight and envy. She was now living out our Banga adventures, while I remained in the imaginary version.

Banga was one of my first encounters with my destiny, opening the door into a world which included lasting friendships, unimaginable change, and unanticipated sorrows —all gifts. Play became practice for the reality I was to manifest.

BIG SISTER

Our personal social environment was formed by my father and his buddies who studied in Italy and who married Italian women. Our families remained a tightly knit community that became my safest place. We were so close that, for a brief time, one of those families lived with us while their house was being built. I was too young to have anything but vague memories of their daughter, barely a toddler, sleeping in a crib by my bed, often waking up at night, standing in her crib and talking for, what felt like, an eternity.

Every morning, I saw my mom give her friend, Rosa, shots in her upper thigh. Years later she told me that the friend suffered from unexplained panic attacks—most likely now we know, due to post-partum depression—and was prescribed daily shots for years. Those were the only two memories I have of their time living in our home, but not long after that, I remember their big move and newly built house. Within a couple of years, they had another daughter and I, enamored with all things baby, was old enough to hold the newborn, a moment memorialized in a photo that I still have.

On the weekends, our moms set up a recurring half-day playdate for the kids, and we alternated weekends at each other's homes. One early morning, our driver from Bangladesh, Joseph, dropped me and May off at Rosa's new house. We rang the doorbell, but no one answered. The main gate was unlocked and so was the front door. Joseph walked in with us, but even after we saw that no one was in the living room or the kitchen, he said before leaving us, "Everybody is still sleeping, they will wake up soon."

After he left, May and I waited in the living room darkened by curtains, for what felt like hours. The silence was interrupted only by my intermittent awareness of the wall clock ticking. Both of us were too young to tell time, however, I was old enough to have our home phone number memorized, which prompted me to locate the phone and call my mom. When I put the handset to my ear I recognized a busy signal, which meant another handset was off the hook in another room, a trick many homes used to prevent the help from making calls when no one was home. I took May's hand and walked up the stairs, hoping either to see someone awake or to find the other phone that was off the hook and call my mom.

I was nervous to walk into their bedrooms. It didn't take long before I realized no one was upstairs; all the beds were made, which meant, no one was home. May and I were alone in a house that was not ours. We were too little to be without an adult. The only comfort was the Italian magazines on the coffee table, and the smell of Italian cooking that, like our home, was also ingrained in the walls of their house.

I wanted to scream but I didn't want to scare May. I looked into her eyes and, still holding her hand, said, "I don't think they are home. We have to call Mamma." May nodded in total trust. She had me to keep her safe. I was her older sister, but I was frightened and worried. My heart was pounding hard, and I was burdened with the sense of responsibility. No time to panic. I had to do what brave characters did in the Japanese anime movies I watched: I had to transform into a superhero for her. If I couldn't do it, I had to put on an act. Once again, my imagination safeguarded me.

We went into each room trying to locate the phone that was off the hook, we were unsuccessful. We didn't dare go into the parents' room—their father had a bad temper and too often we saw him display it—but, I knew we had no choice. I found courage from wanting to reassure my little sister and put my hand on the doorknob of their bedroom: it was locked. I realized the phone was in that room, and I had no way to enter. Although I had no idea when Joseph would return, I told May we ought to go outside and wait on the entrance steps.

The house was new, built in an undeveloped part of the city, where there were no roads, just dirt. It was hot, so hot. The sun was blinding and glistening right above us. We were in the desert, and in the distance, there was only one other home. We saw gerbils pop in-and-out of the ground, and a couple of stray cats walked by us curiously looking for food, which we too wished we had.

My worry grew when I saw a crusty-nosed, bare-footed child with an adult woman, covered from head to toe, approach us out of nowhere through a mirage. She spoke to us in broken Arabic, the kind of Arabic most Saudis used with us, because they suspected we were not Arab—being profiled was something we learned to live with our whole lives. At the time, Italian was my only fluent language and I didn't understand what she said, but she kept signaling with her hand, and murmured in a soft voice for us to go with them. *No! Absolutely not! We will be taken!* I thought as I shook my head.

May looked at me and in Italian said "Let's go with them. I'm hungry!" I looked at the lady and shook my head firmly one last time, after which she and the child walked away.

I don't know why I worried about being taken. The constant fear of personal instability made me doubt and second-guess any situation or environment that did not resemble my own home. Although I didn't sense danger in a potentially harmful and violent way from this woman, I sensed that she was not like me or like my mother and therefore a threat to my sense of security. I didn't want anyone to come back and take us by force, so I took May's hand and walked faster than I could blink, back into the house, locking the door behind us. My fear transformed from feeling alone and sad, to panic that we would never go home. It was the longest day of my life.

When Joseph finally came back at the scheduled time to pick us up, and realized that no one was home, he laughed.

My sob of relief soon turned into rage at his dismissal of our trauma. The 10-minute drive home felt like a road trip. I wanted to run into my mother's arms and scream at her for putting us in this situation. When we finally got to our house, I stormed into the kitchen unsure of whether I should tell her about our day or about Joseph's reaction.

I was trying to swallow the lump in my throat and find my words, "Mamma! No one was there!! We were alone the whole day!" I said as I burst into tears.

As she took off her apron, readying herself to go rest now that we were home, she wacked her forehead and confessed, "Oh, silly me! I forgot Rosa said they were going out of town today."

May was already at the table eating, but I was too upset to take a bite.

Despite the small age difference between May and me, there was a degree of casual naiveté about her. She seemed to have come into this world with a stronger sense of belonging and trust. It is easy, especially now, for me to recount this about her. She didn't seem as troubled, bothered, or concerned with the things that haunted my thoughts. This difference between us has taught me how much nature played a part in my own story. May and I were nurtured the same. We were raised like twins, almost. We had the same rules, the same experiences, the same upbringing, the same love, and the same attention, but our issues as they manifested and unfolded over the years, could not be more different. While I had a shaken trust in what I didn't have control over, May showed an admirable amount of trust in the unknown.

May's trust was tested one summer when we were on the beach of Jesolo in Italy. During our vacation time in this quaint Italian coast beach in the Provence of Venice, we spent our afternoons, until sunset, playing with friends, swimming in the ocean, riding on inflatable boats, building sand-castles, and eating fresh coconut, potato chips, and snow cones.

I was carefree. During those weeks, I lived without worry, fear, or preoccupation. I was surrounded by an authentic community and enjoyed the casual way of doing life which never happened back home. That easy-going calmness was turned upside down one day. We arrived at the crowded beach, everything seemed normal, kids playing and screaming by the shore, women sunbathing topless, grandparents playing crossword puzzles under the umbrellas, and the beach warning flag was yellow, indicating caution. When this had happened before, we'd gone into the water carefully without incident. On this day, the yellow flag should have been red. May and I entered the water, both of us good swimmers since the age of two. Within minutes I saw May pulled by the power of the current that sucked her little body towards the jetty. When I got close to her, I realized that the current was too strong and that she couldn't keep her head above water. The only way to help her was to put her on my shoulders. I was swallowing water as the waves hit my face, and I could barely keep my eyes open. But my hands were firmly holding my sister's knees, keeping her safely on my shoulders and above water. My toes could not touch the bottom of the ocean, but my legs were strong enough to kick in place to keep me afloat. As my head bopped up and down with May sitting wrapped around my neck, I screamed in Italian, "Please save my sister!"

Although I couldn't comprehend the permanence of death, I now had an experience of the primal instinct to survive.

A group of young teenage girls came to our rescue, with their inflatable boat and a rope that they were using to pull kids out of the water and take them to shore. My sister was safe and that's all that mattered to me. As I cloaked a towel around us, I looked up and saw that the beach flag had turned red. Once again May was serene and reassured by the divine outcome, and with a hand in a bag of potato chips, she told our nanny all about it. I, one the other hand, felt like we had just experienced a real life Banga threat.

JUVENESCENCE

I started grade school speaking Italian and English fluently, but very little Arabic, which immediately put me at odds with my new classmates. I was five years old when I started first grade in the big and fancy private school, nothing like the sweet French-Lebanese home-based kindergarten I attended previously for two years, where I also learned a little French. I opened the door of my classroom and stood still, almost frozen, at the sight before me. There were at least twenty girls running wild around the classroom, all of us in the same red uniform. They were laughing, shouting, and speaking Arabic. No teacher in sight. I scanned the room and quickly noticed one girl quietly sitting at her desk; she was lighter complexioned, with strawberry blonde hair.

I darted towards her, sat next to her, and in English said "Hi, I'm Jasmin. I'm Italian."

I noticed her green eyes when she looked at me to answer, "Hi, I'm Arwa. I'm Dutch." Phew. I had a friend. Like me, Arwa was half European and half Middle Eastern. We became each other's safety blanket all the way through high school.

The school I attended had become my second home. I spent twelve years in what, at the time, was the most highly regarded private school in the region. It was owned by then Prince Salman, the King of Saudi Arabia today. The largest percentage of Saudi royal offspring attended the school. Notably the school was for boys and girls, who were segregated in different campuses. School days were Saturday-Wednesday, the weekends consisted of Thursday, and the Islamic holy day, Friday. On the drive to school each morning, Yasser often played DJ, and we listened to the mix tapes he made: The Jacksons, Prince, Phil Collins, Hall & Oats, The Bee Gees, and Survivor, just some of his favorites during the early 80s. Our driver dropped Yasser off first at the boys' gate every morning, while my mom, sister, and I entered together through the girls' gate. My mother was a well-respected and much-loved head English teacher. For the most part, I found school fun and an opportunity to understand who I was and where I belonged.

Once I started school, I knew we were different because I saw how the girls were divided based on cultural and social backgrounds. My sense of belonging was intermittent, and I spent a lot of time physically in packs, but emotionally alone with my thoughts. I don't have a memory of myself without my mind racing constantly. My thoughts were on a hamster wheel —no destination or finish line in sight. Years later, I realized why meditation appealed to me and how it became an indispensable anchor in my life, stopping the wheel from turning and soothing my antic thoughts.

Because I attended the same school for twelve years, I became good friends with many of the girls in my grade. We were divided by unspoken labels. There were the royal family girls, the *Najdi* girls (from the central region of Saudi Arabia, Najd), the *Hijazi* girls (from the western region of Saudi Arabia, Hijaz), the non-Saudi Arab girls (Palestinian, Jordanian, Lebanese, Egyptian, etc.), and the group I belonged to, the "Western" girls— mixed kids with Arab, usually Saudi, fathers and western, usually European, or American, mothers. We were the girls who spoke English, the Americanized girls, the ones who knew about pop-culture and dressed in the coolest and most recent trends, usually underneath our school uniforms or at our frequent, all girls, weekend gatherings. We eventually referred to ourselves as "the *halfies*."

With the *halfies* I came close to being myself. We could talk about our favorite popstars, flip magazines, drool over all the teen heartthrobs, and talk about our summer crushes during our travels. Our friendships were supported by our parents who were also good friends. Some of our dads had been educated together, and our moms had become each other's support system in this foreign land that they now called home.

When I was younger our families socialized together quite often, but as we got older, the teens gathered at a different house on the weekend and the adults would have adult evening parties once a month. I got to go to the teen gatherings that were girls only. We informally rotated locations. The monthly gatherings were usually themed birthdays. Our costume parties brought to life famous movie stars, popstars, comic book heroes and mythical warriors. Cheese curls, chocolate chip cookies, brownies, and mini club sandwiches were dispersed throughout the party room along with Tang, or Kool-Aid if you were at an American home. The first time I tasted buttered popcorn I thought someone had spit in the bowl—the wet soggy texture of the fluffy crunchy popped kernel made me gag.

During my adolescence, my parents became stricter than the other *halfie* parents— following the cultural rules and social laws—which I resented deeply. My sense of loneliness and feeling different became even more intense, as I became isolated physically and emotionally. My development was now in the charge of adults who guarded seemingly impossible cultural mandates. Because I was an adolescent girl, I was barred from the surprises that feed the imagination and inspire ambition and autonomy. These same strictures bonded together many of my peers who have remained friends. I ended up a lone wolf, perhaps in touch with a couple of them, but not part of the vibrant friendship village that still prospers as they have become aunties and uncles to each other's children and share a bond that is fragrant of childhood and adolescent memories.

In Saudi Arabia, the only country in the world where women didn't drive until June of 2018, families of most classes (upper, upper middle, middle and even lower classes) had a live-in driver and maid. Over the decades, we had live-in couples from Pakistan, Bangladesh, The Philippines, and Indonesia. They were part of our family and we depended on them for their services and, sometimes, emotional support.

When my siblings and I were very young, the housekeepers, who were also our nannies, were like aunties and the drivers, like uncles; as we grew older, they became more like sisters and brothers. My parents were full-time professionals which meant that there were cycles in my young life when I spent more time with the help than with my own parents. We learned words in their languages, and they just about perfected Italian and Arabic after being in our home for many years. During the 1980's three different sets of couples, all from the same Filipino family, lived with us at different intervals. Today, I can still say a few basic things in Filipino, I can cuss you out in Filipino, and I feel like I'm around members of my family when I meet Filipinos.

That sensation of relatedness taught me early on that we create our bonds and ties with fellow humans on a much deeper level than genetics. Despite my internal loneliness, I noticed how comfortable I was around people who shared my non-Arab side, like my nannies and my *halfie* friends. My relationship with my paternal relatives was superficial and uncomfortable. My siblings and I were too different from them. My uncles adored us; each time I felt a tap on my shoulder during family gatherings, I turned to see who it was before I noticed my sweet uncle Mohammad suspiciously looking the other way and singing in Arabic, "It's not me it's the little birdie." Before long I caught on and realized this was our special game. Their wives and children however did not share in the same affectionate sentiment. "No, we can't play with these today, they are broken," one of my cousins would say—in imperfect Arabic for my benefit—when I asked to play with her set of plastic pots and pans which looked perfectly intact. My uncle's wives often changed the subject when I walked in the room. I used to think it was because my Arabic was poor, but as my Arabic improved nothing changed on their part, although my perception became linguistically more astute.

Puberty, like with so many things in the Saudi culture, put a stop to our familial assembly. My Saudi relatives lived the traditional Saudi blend of old cultural practices along with fundamental conservative Islamic beliefs. The girls wore long dresses, and the boys, traditional Saudi thobes. The men and women did not socialize in the same space, and there were gender designated living rooms in all homes, including ours for this purpose. Our gatherings with cousins revolved around food, gossip exchanged amongst the older—illiterate—women, and talks of new tailored gowns and shopping excursions. On occasion, the conversation turned to a TV show broadcast on one of the two Saudi public channels, which some of the younger girls happened to watch. But that was the extent of any social, artistic, political, intellectual, or controversial topics in our obligatory weekly gatherings.

One evening, at my uncle Mohammed's home, when I was a tween, my mom, my sister May, and I sat with the aunts and female cousins in the over-the-top floral patterned décor of the ladies living-room—cultural and social segregation included extended-family gatherings—when we heard one of the elder male cousins clear his throat, a signal that a man was about to enter the room and pay his respects; the women were given a few seconds to cover their faces, as required by Wahhabism, one of the most conservative Islamic sects practiced in most Saudi regions.

Women do not cover from the males in their family to whom they cannot be married, such as a father, grandfather, father-in-law, uncle, nephew, brother, and son, but all other males (not including great grandfathers, grandsons, and great uncles) are potential husbands, including a brother-in-law and cousin, and therefore women are expected to be veiled and practice discreet, minimal interactions.

When my elder cousin entered the room, the only ones left uncovered were the prepubescent girls, his mother and sister, as well as my mother, May, and me. From the doorway, he paid his verbal respects to all the elder women and cousins one by one, skipping me and my sister and respectfully greeting my mother, oddly in English, even though she too spoke Arabic.

"Hello *um Yasser*, how are you?" He asked obligatorily, formally referring to my mother as the customs demanded by her status as Yasser's mother.

"I am well. How come you didn't greet my daughters?" she asked in English as to not make a scene in front of the other women.

His response, again in English, still echoes in my ears today, "When your daughters cover, as they should, I will greet them as well."

My stomach turned. It was as if the comment sucked the air from the room. The humiliation was witnessed by all, even those who didn't understand the words exchanged. I knew our relationship changed forever that day. I also knew my identity had inexorably been uncovered just like my rejected, unveiled face.

My mother said nothing the rest of our visit, and I followed her cue. When we got in the car with my father to head home, all she said was, "Aziz, I will not be taking the girls to your brothers' homes anymore. If their uncles want to see them, they can come visit us at our home." My father didn't need to ask what happened, and as the man of few words that he was, he didn't say anything in response. That was the beginning of the end of our relationship with my Arab relatives. Over the years we remained respectfully close to my uncles, and the males maintained cordial relationships with my brother, but that was without question what triggered my personal identity crisis about my belonging and heritage.

My social life was pre-designed by cultural formulas, and my creative side was bound by the lack of outlets and opportunities. Nothing compelled me, challenged my curiosity, or ignited intrigue, until 1983. That was when Michael Jackson's *Thriller* became the biggest selling album of all time. I was hooked from the first time I saw the video clip of his Motown 25 "Billie Jean" performance. I spent hours watching his videos, listening to his music, mimicking him and his sense of style.

Within a short time, I had become the best MJ impersonator of my generation—locally. Michael Jackson and I became synonymous. He represented freedom. He was not bound by his gender or his race but rather presented an infusion of all mirroring aspects of self-expression. He was a singer, a dancer, a performer, an entertainer, a storyteller, a fashionista, and a humanitarian. I was thrilled. The world of dance and artistic expression became the one constant I had to fall back on—always in the privacy of my bedroom or small social gatherings with girlfriends—for comfort, escape and survival.

In the bathroom I used several products in an attempt to hold a couple of shiny Jheri curls, but my fine straight hair did not cooperate. "Can I get a perm?" I finally asked my mom one day, "I don't think so, you're too young and it's expensive," was her reply. I flashed back to the time she had a stunning salon-styled Afro in the late 1970s but didn't have the courage to challenge her. When the King of Pop shockingly passed away in 2009, at age 50, I received messages and phone calls from relatives and friends I hadn't spoken to in years. Apparently, I was the first person they thought of when they heard the news. I mourned his passing because he was a symbolic embodiment of my aspirations during the most challenging parts of my adolescence.

My love for dance and music consumed the greatest part of my tween and teen years. With no freedom and a great deal of time on my hands, I spent my days and nights playing music, composing on the keyboard and piano, writing songs, and dancing. By the mid-eighties breakdance and the whole pop-lock phenomenon had also made its way secretly to Saudi Arabia. It was taboo, but young kids my age were spinning and moonwalking devotedly, like most other teens and preteens around the world. The Michael Jackson explosion was so powerful, and in a country that had never seen anything from the West invade with such impact (not even Elvis and The Beatles had made their way to the desert of the Kingdom), it was viewed as a threat by the elders and especially the conservatives. On the rare occasion that I went to the cassette stores with my mom, I spent all my money on Michael Jackson merchandise. I still remember the time we walked into the *747 Stereo Store* by our house and saw no trace of Michael Jackson anywhere. I was confused and felt a pit in my stomach; I knew this was a bad sign. Within a year any-and-all traces of Michael Jackson in stores (cassettes, posters, and memorabilia) were destroyed and erased by the *Mutawa*, the religious police of Saudi Arabia, officially known as The Committee for the Promotion of Virtue and the Prevention of Vice.

Many of us continued to be devoted MJ fans but had to find ways to safely smuggle his music and videos into the country without being caught. Having ties and a friendship with members of the royal family afforded us such advantages. For a couple of years during that timeframe, my best friend at school was the daughter of then Crown Prince Abdullah bin Abdulaziz, the former King of Saudi Arabia who passed away in 2015. Maha and her three sisters were a new friendship that filled the void of the separation from the co-ed gatherings that my parents imposed. Most of my *halfie* friends were meanwhile still experiencing those co-ed gatherings adjunct to the girls-only gathering. I spent many weekends at the royal compound, where my brother too went to visit Maha's half-brothers, each set of full siblings living in a different palace with their respective mothers. It was easy to become friends with Maha because she had no full-blooded brothers. In her home, where she lived with her mother, Princess al-Anoud, there were no boys, only her three sisters and a very large number of nannies, drivers, and servants.

My weekends at the royal palace began with a drive in our Buick, from my home to the main gates of the royal compound, where we passed several Mercedes and a Rolls Royce parked in the exposed garage and cobble-stone driveway. There was an Olympic size pool, ATVs, horses, movie rooms, and my personal favorite: a discotheque! We spent hours choreographing Michael Jackson dances, breakdance routines, and we even took on the nicknames Ozone and Turbo from the cult movie *Breakin'* starring another one of my biggest heroes, the late Adolfo "Shabbadoo" Quinones. Yet when I put on a fedora and glove and did my "Billie Jean" routine, I came to life and, by request, often entertained Princess Al-Anoud and all her friends. I was ten or eleven years old, but I felt like a star, so alive and so fulfilled.

During that era, I met King Abdullah several times. He came to visit his daughters on some weekends, often while I too was there. He was charming, humble, and kind. Like my father, his mother was from the Saudi region in the northern part of the country, Hail. After kissing his daughters, he would turn to me and say, "Come here and say hello, my little cousin," a reference to our regional connection. His blue-grey eyes resembled my uncle Mohammad's eyes, and his Van Dyke beard looked a lot like my eldest uncle's. I was shy around him, and back then didn't realize how important he really was. Having such intimate interactions with the royal family was not unusual because the family is large in numbers and in influence. They were privileged to pick and choose their favorites and who they wanted to befriend. I knew I was a favorite to Maha and her family because I was westernized, which they were too. They were liberal, educated, modern, and strong women. We had a lot in common, although socially, we were worlds apart, a fact that did not escape the notice of my father.

My parents did not oppose my friendship with the royal sisters, nor my brother with the royal princes. However, once I passed that official puberty threshold, so many things in my life changed. As a teenager instant gratification took a hold of my decision-making, and my parents knew the permanence of those impulsive choices. My mother and father could foresee the dangers of such influential friends. One can find themselves socially almost imprisoned by all the restrictions and implications. Especially women. No commoner can refuse a request or demand from a member of the royal family, whether as a potential spouse, or inner circle friend. Maha didn't know how my parents' felt, and I was too embarrassed to say anything about it, because I knew she did not subscribe to that way of thinking or the default political monarchist way of life. Two years after the start of my exciting and adventurous friendship with the future King's daughters, my parents decided it was no longer a good fit and asked me to slowly minimize my contact with the young princess. They knew what I did not, that a deep friendship between members of the royal family and the professional classes was not sustainable. My parents were not wrong in their worry; it was in fact at the palace where I saw my first porno video. After choreographing a breakdance routine in the discotheque one afternoon, Maha and I joined her older sister and friends in the TV room, where they were watching a French movie, a language they were fluent in. The girls were all giggling, but I was clueless. Within a few minutes the scene of two naked women performing oral sex in a shower brought to life silly laughter in the room. My heart was racing, and my throat felt tight. I was confused and scared. Maha exclaimed, casually, "Our auntie who visits from Jordan loves these movies, we always find them in her room." The horror on my face was confirmed when she asked, "Oh no! have you not seen a movie like this before?!"

Eventually Maha and her sisters switched schools, which made the parting easier, but I was angry, sad, hurt, upset, and didn't quite understand why I had to let go of our friendship. I saw Maha years later, in college. She was warm and affectionate and immediately invited me over to the palace for an evening party she was hosting. "It's so good to see you, you haven't changed at all! I really miss you!" she said genuinely after a tight hug. I was equally happy to see her, but lovingly declined the invitation because my life was so different from hers that it would not have made sense to rekindle a childhood friendship, one that my parents predicted would remain a happy memory and that now had me more aware of my own forming political and social opinions. More recently—during King Abdullah's last months of life and reign—I was saddened and disturbed by the news that Maha and her sisters were captives in their own homes, held by their half-brothers, confirming my own point of view of a system I could not embrace. There was limited information and only a few videos on the internet of the four Saudi princesses and their alarming conditions. I was keenly aware of the mysteries surrounding people's private lives, where it is not unusual to accept the silence following an unexplained disappearance. I still ache at the thought of their destiny and unknown fate.

School remained interesting as long as new students arrived. In Middle School, one of those students was Reem. She and I became best friends instantly; we spent hours late at night on the phone to plan our matching outfits for school the next day. We had to be creative since we wore mandatory uniforms, but it became fun to match hair ribbons, sock colors, shoe styles, and often even whole outfits underneath our uniforms. Reem and I talked about music, boys, movies, and school, but what we talked about the most was gender equality.

We were both strong and opinionated young women. Reem's mom is the toughest Saudi woman I have ever met. I idolized her growing up. In many ways I saw in her the kind of Saudi woman that my Italian mother could not be but that I wanted to be. I identified with auntie Wafa because she and I had an Arab childhood, as well as shared progressive social ideals. I thought of her as a rebel, and a total badass.

Saudi mothers are addressed as "mother-of-the-*oldest*-son." If the oldest child is not a son, then she is addressed as "mother-of-the-*first*-son." If she does not have a son, then she is addressed as "mother-of-the-son-you-would-have-had-and-named-after-the-paternal-grandfather." Auntie Wafa had four daughters and one son. Her oldest child was my best friend, Reem. She never answered to being called "mother-of-Mansour (her only son, and second child)," and instead insisted on being called "mother-of-Reem." This told me everything about how assertive a woman can be, and how it was acceptable to be a female in the world without hiding apologetically. Reem's father was from the same hometown as my father, and while her mother was Saudi, she was raised in a progressive and liberal family. Reem's parents gained their education in the west, and her father is a man I deeply admire because he was able to take his educational opportunities and break the cycle of patriarchal rule in his own nuclear family. Reem and her three sisters and one brother were all given equal chances at a liberal and westernized education after high school, outside of Saudi Arabia.

Even though we were young, we were both aware of the subtleties that our parents displayed in their social behaviors. In the privacy of our interactions, we spoke about the cultural struggles, but in public, at school, we took every opportunity to be carefree tweens and teens, at times assimilating just to blend in.

"Ricciolina!" I would exclaim when I saw her at school in the morning. *Ricciolina*, Italian for curly haired girl, was my name for her. "Let me see your socks!!" I asked to make sure we were matching, as we each ran to our respective classes.

"*Jasmin!*" She would squeal in excitement with her perfectly huge and beautiful smile, showing off our matching socks and black boots.

Reem matched me in more ways than just our fashion statements. We were intellectual counterparts.

Distractions had become my way of thriving. Besides Michael Jackson, music, and hanging out with my friends, my other joyful escape was the time spent in Italy with my Nonni (grandparents), Zia and Zio (my aunt and her husband, my uncle), as well as my two cousins—who were more like older brothers—and the many friends in the neighborhood.

The school year passed slowly and painfully compared to the speed of summer months when we were in Italy tasting freedom and a sense of normalcy. We toured my mom's beautiful country of birth. In my childhood, I saw Italy north to south and east to west. We rented apartments with my grandparents, aunt, uncle, and cousins along the gorgeous east Mediterranean Sea coast or on the Lake Garda not far from where my relatives live. As a child I became familiar with the works of art we visited in the many cathedrals, museums, monuments, and piazzas. I was in awe of the country I proudly claimed as my own. I was proud of being Italian. I loved the people, the food, and the land. I felt at home in Italy, even though my time there each summer was too short to feel like I fully belonged. In Italy, we didn't stand out like we did in Saudi. We spoke like natives, looked like locals, and soaked up the riches as tourists. We were well versed in modern Italian pop culture, and not just the operatic works of art and folklore.

My happiest memories are the days spent at our family farm in the northern part of Italy, a town called Botticino, not far from Milan, in the province of Brescia where my family lived. Out of my siblings, I was the only one with a strong country-life gene. I loved helping my Zia check on and feed the chickens as well as gather the eggs each morning. I felt alive going through the vineyard and vegetable garden to pick zucchini and green beans. The evening dinner time was the culmination of the days' activities, with fresh baked polenta and gorgonzola, zucchini frittata made with the very eggs I collected and zucchini I picked, and sometimes frying battered zucchini flowers, all enjoyed over the large marble table, under the huge white mulberry tree. There was nothing wild, luxurious, or extravagant about our summer vacations, especially compared to all our friends in Saudi who, like us, escaped to Europe and the United States. Theirs were five-star trips to lavish resorts and summer boarding schools. I did not envy them, but often felt like I had fewer stories to share when we reunited at school in the fall. Nonetheless, I was always excited to relive my Italian life through the many photographs that I took and the souvenirs I brought home. It sustained me during the school year.

Life is simple and togetherness is priceless; this was my story with my Italian relatives. There were no lines that separated us, we were one. I knew that I belonged. We were a talkative bunch, as the elders shared their narrative of generations past, I learned from the family that my great aunt Maria, the nun, and I shared many similarities in our looks and manners. My cousins, Vincenzo—known as Vince (pronounced *Vinche*) due to the fact that it was a family name and there were several Vincenzo elders—and Franco, were the coolest young men I knew. They were smart, funny, and I looked up to them in total adoration. I loved meeting their girlfriends and listened in awe when they told stories of their time in the mandatory military draft training, as well as of their many travels. I remain close to my eldest cousin, Vince. Without him, I am not sure my story would be the one that I have to tell today. I didn't realize, and it didn't matter, that my aunt's in-laws were not related to me by blood. Her husband's cousins Mario and Luigi (real names!) entertained us along with their father, Zio Vincenzo, under the white mulberry tree playing the mandolin, guitar, and accordion as we all sang along to old Italian folk songs.

I was always eager to impress and please my Nonno Franco, whose opinion mattered to me. Thoughtful and guarded, he taught me so much. He was known for telling endless stories, and even though others joked about that behind his back, I was glued to him in anticipation of the moral that was always at the end of a longwinded monologue. I learned about humility and discretion from my favorite story he often told, the one about "Quello lí" (Italian for "that one").

My Nonno would start off recounting, "That man loves to point! At the vegetable market he asks the vendor to bag it up, and the vendor asks, *which one?* The man replies loudly, *Quello lí, quello lí*, as he points at the tomatoes!" Nonno gestured with his pinky.

"Why did he do that, Nonno?" I asked every time, as if hearing the story for the first time.

"Naturally, he wanted everyone to look his way because it was impossible to not notice the huge jewel on his ring," he would say in an unimpressed tone. "It was obvious he wanted to be admired," he continued, rolling his eyes. Vanity was a pet-peeve of my Nonno.

My Nonna Teresa shared not only her name but also her big compassionate heart with the saint from Calcutta, and I learned that about her by watching her generosity with everyone. She gave me gelato money when we left the house, but it was her unconditional and devoted attention when I talked to her that made me feel adored. Despite her hearing loss, she listened attentively and asked me to speak louder; I knew she didn't want to miss a word of what I was saying. My happy place was sitting with her in the living room after lunch, while I watched music videos and she did the crossword puzzles wearing her large reading glasses, falling intermittently into mini naps.

Zia Flora was the life of the party and the bosom of the family. My sister May and I were very close to our aunt. She took the two of us to Lake Garda every summer on cruise ship tours, sightseeing, shopping, eating pizza and giggling at all the silly encounters on the train, bus and on foot. It was easy to forget all the troubles that brewed in our unstable way of growing up. I learned how to dream and fantasize thanks to my Zia, who taught me the power of attitude and spontaneity, and knew how to model it to her nieces.

"Let's go to the record store on Sunday, and then go to Pinco Pallino for gelato. We'll take the bus at 14:30," she would say with the enthusiasm of a teenage girl.

"Grazie Zia!! Can we also go to La Standa?" I asked eagerly referring to the chain department store, owned by Berlusconi.

"You bet! Let's get all your school supplies while we're there!" She replied, handing me spending money and winking.

My Italian childhood was so lucky and so uncommon.

At the end of each summer, it was always so hard to say goodbye to my family, to Italy, to my freedom.

LOSS

Besides music and dance, I loved animals. I spent hours behind our walled-in yard soliciting the attention of stray cats and observed the rare and infrequent appearances of birds, which were scarce in the treeless desert of the city. Even before I could read, my kindergarten French teacher gave me an Italian encyclopedia of animals which I still keep and preserve like an antique. I flipped through the whole thing daily, page by page, looking at all the different animals. Starting from my 4-year-old illiterate visual observations, I learned in detail about mammals, reptiles, insects, birds, and marine life. I kept my own menagerie of stuffed animals that I treated like live pets and took my invisible dog on daily walks.

Pets are not common in Saudi Arabia. Some families had a cat or two, maybe an exotic caged bird, and for decor, large fish tanks. My mother was not a fan of animals in the home, even though my dad, like me, had a great love for dogs. But dogs especially are not kept as pets in Saudi Arabia because according to the Islamic teachings and some interpretations, they are considered "filthy" animals and belong outside as guards. Some Muslims believe that the angels don't enter a home to receive one's prayers if a dog is present. My parents did not subscribe to this particular philosophy, but nonetheless, my mom refused to have animals in the home. For a short time, we had a hamster, a couple of small water turtles, and several generations of stray cats outside in the yard.

A mama cat had a litter of kittens in the closet of our housekeeper's trailer-house within the confines of our walled-in property. The cat must have snuck in through the window one afternoon when no one was in the trailer. My mom, who meant well—but made no secret of that fact that she was against animals in the house—asked the housekeeper to find a box, place the one-day old kittens in it, and leave them outside of the trailer for the mama cat to find upon her return from her hunt for food.

From the nature documentaries I watched and my minimal reading over the years about animal behavior, I knew that wild animals are instinctive, and that the mama cat would probably not recognize her kittens if someone handled them and removed them from where she left them.

I begged my mom not to let the housekeeper touch the kittens, "Their mama won't recognize them, and they will die if she doesn't take care of them!"

"It will be fine; we will place the kittens where she can see them. They can't be in the closet, the housekeepers need their room to be free of this hassle," she said, in defense of her stance.

"Please, trust the mama cat, she will move them out on her own when she sees there is a lot of action around their spot," I insisted, but my plea went unheard.

The kittens cried in the box while their mama, just inches away, cried too. It was clear she was grieving the loss of the kittens she no longer recognized, and that she was not going to care for them, so I took it upon myself to become their mom.

I made a soft and warm bed for them and placed them in the outdoor pool bathroom of our home. It was December, and even though winters are brief and mild in Saudi Arabia, the desert nights can be brutally frigid. I rushed home every day from school to syringe-feed the kittens powdered milk, one by one; I did the same every morning before school and every night before bed. They did not survive. All three kittens died within a week, and I was gut punched. To those around me, the incident was not a source of sorrow, although they tried to comfort me.

The death of *my* kittens marked the beginning of my long journey through loss and grief. Loss became a formidable teacher from an early age, and the lessons it offered remained with me through adulthood.

As a young child, I was frequently plagued by cold sweat running down my spine, or my hair standing up on top of my head, such was my vulnerability to the forces of chance. Early on, I adopted a stance of fight or flight. Many years later I recognized this—I was in a constant state of biological emergency, always guarding against loss of people, places, animals, my own self.

I focused on the unwarranted notion that I could, at any moment, lose my mother because she was a cultural outsider, an Italian. But I was also never far from thoughts of my father dying, perhaps because I knew he was the anchor in our lives, the one true Saudi in the family who legitimately belonged there. Our sense of security depended on him. If he wasn't there, then my mother's sojourn would come to a legal end, and my sense of pending impermanence would become a reality. What would that mean for me?

As a maturing teenager I had frequent flashbacks, one in particular when I was in first grade. Each year our school put on an end-of-the-year extravagant production of theater performances, music, traditional dance, and athletic exhibitions for the King, who on occasion attended these celebrations along with other distinguished men in society and the fathers of students. Because our schools were segregated, only kindergarten-fourth grade girls were allowed to participate in the boys' event. Both my brother and sister were also part of this event. My father attended, and I knew he was in the audience sitting in bleachers around the huge soccer field of the boys' section of our school. It was impossible to spot my father in the crowd, but I stared at the hundreds of seated men, all dressed the same, and held my breath, hoping to see him.

In my red athletic Adidas outfit, holding a small hula hoop above my head, I walked on the soccer field in choreographed precision, where all the students—kindergarten to high school—were also performing. The marching band's music was deafening, the stadium lights were blinding, and as a youngster, my limited view deprived me from seeing the grand display on the stadium field. I was excited to be out late at night because I felt like a grown-up. I didn't want to admit to myself, however, that I was afraid of the swarming crowd both on the field and in the stadium seats.

A young man in the choir collapsed. He probably fainted from stage fright or dehydration. A group of students rushed to his aid. This happened quickly, without affecting the flow of the song and dance, and most likely unnoticed by the audience. I was unable to identify the young man, and yet was—illogically—convinced it was my father because, after all, all men who dressed in Saudi clothes looked like my father. I could see my brother Yasser singing in the younger boys' choir, and every time I'd pass close enough to make eye contact with him, he smiled and waved enthusiastically. His lack of concern failed to reassure me.

Reliving these events exacerbated my constant state of alertness.

My parents chose to have another child after a seven-year hiatus. When my mom was four months pregnant, I faced the first terrifying family loss. My father was in Italy on a business trip. It was the weekend. My siblings and I each had a different birthday party to attend that afternoon. After lunch my mom went to take her usual nap. But on this afternoon, I had a feeling something was wrong when she stayed in her room longer than expected. I knocked on her door, and when she didn't answer, I went in. She was in bed, under the covers, crying.

"Mamma, are you ok?" I asked her, somewhat afraid to hear her answer.

She didn't reply at first. When I approached closer and asked again, she said "Call our doctor and tell him to come with an ambulance."

My hands were shaking as I searched through our family phone book in my parents' bedroom, looking for the number. The doctor's wife answered, and I told her my mom was in bed, not well, and that she needed the doctor right away. He arrived swiftly, and in the ambulance carried my mother to the hospital.

I don't think my siblings thought any of this was a big deal. They didn't seem concerned. I heard my brother ask my mom if he could still go to his party as she was being lifted into the ambulance, to which she said, "Yes, of course, you should all go to your parties, I'll be fine."

My brother and sister went to their parties, but I couldn't, and didn't. My mom stayed in the hospital that night, and I watched the maid Ella clean the blood-soaked sheets and mattress. Ella noticed the look on my face and said in her Tagalog inflected English, "Your mama is not going to have a baby, but don't be scared, she is going to be ok."

I wanted to know what was actually going to happen to my mother. I wished my father were here. I ended up distracting myself by staring at the TV screen, watching *Scooby Doo*, and waiting by the phone, hoping my father would call. To help me feel better, Ella said we should have a party to celebrate my mom's safe recovery. She made a Betty Crocker yellow cake and peach tang. To this day, when I drink peach juice, I think of that mournful and scary day.

My Mom's miscarriage was a turning point. I bounced between the relatively carefree space of childhood and the pending acknowledgement of maturity, which included birth, death, and everything in between—marriage.

Marrying young is the norm, usually after high school or during early college years, with a post-honeymoon pregnancy. Babies effectively distract young mothers who have few opportunities for creative endeavors. My parents made it clear that was not their expectation, and I was not eager to grow up so fast.

Most of my friends and cousins were thinking of their future married life since they were tweens. By the time they were teenagers, that fantasy was becoming more of a reality. The only time I had thought of marriage was when I was a very little girl, still clueless of what marriage was. I loved playing house, only May and I changed it to "Airplane." Our bunk beds were transformed into an airplane cabin, where she and I were traveling women with our newborn baby dolls, on a long flight to meet our husbands in another city. During the flight, which was enhanced with a blowing fan by our side to simulate the noisy flight experience, I would turn to May, who was in the seat next to me, and introduce myself, "I am Angela, I am on my way to meet my husband," showing off my husband's picture in my wallet—a photograph clipping from an Italian magazine of Julio Iglesias. As we experienced turbulence during our very long flight (no destination named) we nursed and changed our babies' diapers repeatedly. This game distracted me from the fact that I was born into a culture that allowed women little room for personal independence and from the fear that I would never blossom outside of my bedroom.

Puberty and I did not hit it off. Rapid changes were happening in my body chemistry as well as the emotional cosmos of my intellect. Being the middle child also added to my self-awareness and confusion. I was a younger and an older sibling, but I was also the oldest girl, which meant bigger responsibilities. I was becoming aware of real life, which included mortality.

One of the rare summers that we did not go to Italy, we received disturbing news from my relatives that my beloved Nonno was in the hospital being treated for serious pulmonary failure. I don't remember my parents sharing much with us, but I heard my mom on long distance calls with my Italian relatives. Just days after that initial call, on a hot August, Arabian evening, while I was in our swimming pool under bright stars, my mom came to give me the devastating news, "Nonno Franco has died," she said abruptly before going back into the house.

The news stunned me. I didn't really know what or how to feel. His was the first human death I could grasp. My paternal grandmother died before my father married, and his father died when I was only six. I knew him and liked him, but he was already very old when I was born, and because he lived in another city, I may have seen him only a few times before he passed away. I never really knew him well enough to love and appreciate him as I had my Italian grandfather. At six, I was unfazed by the death of an old person. My Saudi grandfather was in his 90s if not older. As an adolescent, however, I was aware of mortality and distraught at the thought of never seeing my Nonno again.

In my tweens, all the big, scary questions had started to make their way into my consciousness. After my mom shared the news and headed back in the house, I felt as if it were a dream. I swam to the bottom of the pool holding my breath as long as I could and fighting back any tears and invasive thoughts. This was my introduction to grief, an alien feeling that I had invented for myself—while my mom was aloof as she mourned her departed father. Silent, tenderly sad, and private.

A month after his passing, I dreamed about my Nonno, a dream about our life at the family farm in Botticino, a place of comfort and joy, Nonno's place. He was wearing his country clothes, and my cousins and siblings walked past him, as if he weren't there. I watched myself in a dream where Nonno was alive. My Nonno watched as I tried to get the attention of my cousin Vince who walked past us without acknowledging me or our invisible Nonno. A few seconds of desperate confusion that in a dream went by slowly, my Nonno finally looked deeply into my soul with his tender grey eyes, smiled and said, "You are not mistaken, I am in fact dead, this is a dream, but I am here for a reason. Only you can see me right now and I have a few things to tell you. I know you love this place the same way I did because it is a reminder of what is beautiful about nature, family, and life. I know you are going to make some bold decisions in your life and pursue your dreams unapologetically. I trust you will stay on this path as you become an adult. Continue being a respectful daughter even if you are rebellious and daring. Stay connected to nature in all the ways you can. Don't doubt yourself. *Sei una brava bambina*. You are a good girl."

I woke up in a startle. These were Nonno's words, spoken only in a dream.

Eighth graders are right in the middle, not quite children, nor cool high schoolers yet. In Saudi Arabia, when I was growing up, school consisted of six years of elementary, three years of middle school, and three years of high school. I was in the middle of the middle school years, a very lost and somewhat socially insignificant stage. I was not excited to go back to school after the summer I just had, in part, because unlike all my friends who had traveled to Europe and America, I had remained home. This was one of the few summers we did not travel because my parents were working on major home remodeling and construction. I didn't have fancy new fashion items to show off or secret stories of new crushes. When you grow up in an oppressed society like we did, the vacation trips are what we lived for and the charge that kept us going all year until the next big trip. From my end, I was stuck and left behind in the previous summer. Remembering how each summer we smuggled magazines and posters when we reentered the country. How I hid video tapes and music cassettes under feminine products and undies in the suitcases, to discourage the customs agents from searching. This summer I had little to share, I didn't participate in the secretive poster and video exchange parties, and I resented being left out. I had nothing to contribute: my *infidel* grandfather died.

That same summer, while we were tiptoeing around multiple house projects, our housekeepers and driver went back to the Philippines to visit their families, so my sister and I were expected to do house chores. Begrudgingly, I learned how to make my bed, clean the bathroom, fold my laundry, and wash dishes. Nevertheless, I learned life skills and faced the reality of how the rest of the world worked.

After what felt like the longest summer of my life, I returned to school filled with dread. I was unwittingly walking into a painful awakening. My friend Jamila shouted, "*Oh my god!* I think she's here!" as she ran toward a major commotion across the building. She ran and I followed her, asking who we were looking for.

"Nebras!" she yelled without looking back.

Why the excitement to see Nebras? A year older than us, she was a close family friend of Jamila's and someone whom we often ran into at school and shared small talk with. She was an energetic and spunky girl, with black hair that could rival Rapunzel's in length. I didn't know her intimately, but I was always in awe of her animated presence and friendly disposition. As we ran through the corridors of the high school building, I saw a classroom with girls huddled over Nebras.

"Jamila! She's here!" I called to my friend.

An older girl snapped aggressively, "This is not a show! What do you want?! Why are you here?"

I was shocked at that aggressive confrontation. But when we moved closer to Nebras, I broke out into a cold sweat, a signal that this was serious. Nebras was a frail, thin and unrecognizable little girl. She was wearing a wool hat, and in a fatigued but affectionate tone she said hello to both Jamila and me. She was sitting at her desk, clearly happy to be at school.

Nebras was sick. Everyone came back from the summer looking bigger, and yet, she looked smaller. I couldn't see her long ponytail. Her hat seemed to cover a bald head. She had no eyebrows.

It was my first encounter with cancer.

Before this day, I had never heard of cancer. Although I had a visual of diseases which terrorized me through pictures of animals with growths and tumors in my mother's medical encyclopedia—and which triggered an early onset of hypochondria—I was paralyzed at the thought that cancer was a tumor you couldn't always see. Nebras had just come back from the United States where she was receiving treatment for an aggressive brain tumor. She had lost all her beautiful hair, and her personality was replaced with a calm and wise soul, one that is rare to see in a child. She was more like an elderly grandmother, than a feisty teenager. I felt awe and sadness. Then it struck me: while I was complaining about my crappy summer at home, Nebras was fighting for her life through chemotherapy and radiation treatments in a land far away from home. I know that I experienced some misplaced guilt and shame. I realized in that moment that there are real catastrophes in this world and they don't all revolve around me.

Nebras continued to attend classes on the days that she felt well enough. One afternoon at the end of the school day, I saw her sitting by herself, and I mustered the courage to approach. I was breathing rapidly, my heart pounding in my chest, the familiar cold sweat running down my spine, caressing my back. I was confronting a fear, and Nebras was the embodiment of that fear. When I drew near, I smiled and quietly asked her how she was doing. She answered, "I can't complain, the grace of Allah is with me. All is well."

I didn't quite have the words for it, but that encounter turned my awareness upside-down. During that same period, my mother had begun to introduce me to her newfound passion of New Age teachings. What seemed suspiciously hypothetical mumbo jumbo out of my mom's mouth and from the books she read, was suddenly epitomized in Nebras. I was inspired by her strong will and total peace. She was delicate and kind. She seemed to speak like a grown up, not a young girl who is facing great suffering and her untimely death.

I went home that afternoon feeling surprisingly happy about the fact that I had the courage to talk to her. I couldn't stop thinking about her and how she responded. I so often lived in my own thoughts, harassed, and sometimes bullied by those personified fears and worries. This unusual feeling of peace and awe was a welcome replacement. I was relieved that I was ok with what I didn't fully understand; this encounter marked the beginning of the lifelong lesson of letting go. I had two minutes alone with Nebras and offered sympathy in exchange for needed and effective inspiration.

Her serenity in the face of serious illness and her unwavering faith have never left me. Somehow, I had this naive trust that she was going to be okay because she was at peace with her destiny. Nebras was hospitalized two weeks later. Jamila planned to visit her every day after school. She brought her George Michael posters to cheer her up. I could not process what was happening and felt like I had no one to talk to about it. I felt confused, angry, sad, and even desperate. I tried to listen to music, compose and dance as a distraction, but it rarely worked during this somber unfolding.

Those days dragged on forever, and yet sped by in a flash, eventually culminating in news of Nebras' passing. The feeling of anguish remained with me for decades. I was no longer oblivious to the impermanence of this life. I become overwhelmed by fear at the thought of getting sick and dying—myself. From mild to severe hypochondria, I developed anxiety, and a temporary case of hidden depression. My family was not fully aware of my pain, although my mother had an inkling. She wrote it off as teenage drama and hormones, having had no experience with such troubles herself as a young teenager.

But my pain was real. I had begun to understand the fragility of life.

School was a distraction during this challenging time. I was not as social as I normally would be, but I tried to engage in situations that pulled me away from dwelling in thoughts of sadness and despair. In class I chatted with friends and passed notes when the teacher could not see. We snuck snacks into our hungry bellies since our only food break was a half hour early in the morning after which food was not allowed in the classroom. Lamia, the girl who sat next to me in class, passed me a note *Do you want a snickers bar?* I looked at her somewhat confused, she shrugged and pointed to Arwa, my Saudi-Dutch friend, indicating who had passed her the note for me. Lamia sat between us, passing our notes during class. It surprised me that she participated since she was such a studious and quiet girl. She was a transfer student from one of the public schools and had been with us less than a couple of years, but it didn't take long for her to find her place, even in her introverted way. We never got Lamia in trouble as the note pigeon, but Arwa and I got caught a few times sneaking food into our mouths and passing notes to one another. Getting in trouble was fun because class was so boring.

Two months after Nebras died, I was sitting in the science lab at school where we were unusually quiet as we waited for our teacher to show up. I already had notes written and ready to pass to Arwa. Lamia was not yet in class. When our Sudanese science teacher finally entered the classroom, twenty minutes late, she took one look and turned around, crying. Although no one seemed surprised by her behavior, I didn't get it.

I muttered, "What's going on?"

My classmate, Amal, turned and whispered to me, "Lamia died," words that fogged my thinking and made me doubt my hearing.

I asked again, "What is going on?"

She continued, "Lamia died in a car accident over the weekend."

But Lamia was so *alive*, stunningly beautiful, and very smart, a good sport about passing our notes, a quiet conversant with a dimple inflected smile. It seemed impossible that another healthy and vibrant child was gone in one instant. There was nothing, not even *Allah*, that could save us. Why did we exist?

Our science teacher could not come back to the classroom, so our homeroom teacher came in instead and formally shared the news of Lamia's death. The teacher offered some gentle words of sorrow and a prayer for Lamia's departed soul and her grieving family. Lab was dismissed and we went back to our classroom to read the Koran. The only public grieving that I saw expressed around me was the traditional Islamic mourning, where the Koran is recited, and prayers are offered constantly. Chants about our mortality and weakness in the face of God's will were expressed often by everyone, but I was not consoled. I was desperate. I yearned for a greater understanding, and I wanted to come to terms with all of this without hating life—*God* (which I was already doubting existed).

I sank into a quieter state of anxiety and my slumbers were filled with nightmares and night sweats. I always shared a bedroom with my sister during our childhood, but in adolescence I had my own bedroom. One night after a string of nightmares, a panic attack, and, to my shock, wetting the bed, I woke my mother and told her I was scared to be alone. At 2 am both my mom and I dragged my sister May with her mattress into my room. The next day, May officially moved back into our joint bedroom that we continued to share till the day I left the home.

My mom—who was now almost cult-ishly involved in the New Age movement of Positive Thinking—was blossoming spiritually. She was available to her children, but also distracted by her awakened appetite to feed and satiate her rousing soul. I knew she was there for me in my every moment of need, but part of me also felt ashamed to appear weak and frail, and I kept many of my haunted and damaging thoughts to myself, as well as the frequent panic attacks that I soothed with deep breathing and music. My moping around with a subtle and dimmed presence, however, was obvious and becoming a concern to my mom and teachers.

Wrapped in her night robe, my mom sat on the couch next to my curled body before going to bed, and said, "Do you recognize how beautiful and rich your life is? Do you see how you are missing out on all the joys by succumbing to the thoughts of the sad events that recently transpired?" I didn't respond. She tried again and insisted in her confident new-age-positive-thinking tone, "Even when there is loss of life in the world, there is new life coming in. If you enjoy the gift of this life, you can overcome the sadness of the losses." She meant well. I appreciated her efforts, but nothing that she said made a bit of difference to my suffering. I was a sensitive child, grappling with the meaning of death. There seemed to be no validation that my thoughts were *normal.*

The next day at school, our homeroom teacher entered the classroom, closed the door, and said, "I have been asked by several of your parents to talk to you. You have all endured a couple of very painful and scary events recently. It is not easy and believe me when I say: I really do understand how you all feel. You are still here, so do you want to make the best of what days, months and hopefully years you have left? What do you think your friends who have passed would be doing if they were here today?" My classmates and I sat silently and meek, listening to her every word. "You all must trust *Allah* and understand you have a purpose on earth, you will discover this purpose and you will embody it. Don't wait till you are a grown up to seek," she continued. "We are here to live the human experience as *Allah* intended, in all stages of our lives, which includes death. To be what *Allah* wants us to be is not something reserved for our adulthood; it is meant to be from the moment we are born. It is who you are, not what you will do, or become. I encourage you to find the strength to push forward and reflect the image of the prophet Mohammad in his patience and acceptance. When you feel scared and lost, reach out, talk to someone you trust and always call upon *Allah* and your faith."

Her words took me by surprise. And my feelings were validated.

While she invited us to call upon the *Islamic Allah*, I translated that to mean "my higher self." This pep talk was not the cultural norm even with its Islamic inflections—at all. She sounded like a Western motivational speaker, and although I have heard progressive Muslim clerics talk that way, she did not sound like a teacher in a conservative Muslim school in the 1980s. She displayed the kind of wisdom that should, ideally, inform every teacher; her strength and inspirational approach gave me a calming reassurance—a taste of hope and courage once again. This was a halting moment. Even though it did not "fix" things or change the facts, it certainly gave me the strength to crawl out of the deep well I had fallen into.

My teacher's pep-talk validated my mom's intentions, which I realized I had dismissed because she was my mother, and because she bypassed the sorrow. After school, when I went home and told my mom about it, she smiled, as if to say *it's finally time*. She handed me a book and said, "I think you are mature enough to handle this book. Read it, and we can talk about it. I think it could change your life in more ways than you can anticipate."

The book is still on my nightstand, and I have read it more times than I can count. I continue to seek and find all the reassuring motivation I need when I read it.

Amid loss, I have learned that "You Can Heal Your Life," just like Louise Hay did, and promised, in that life-changing book I was handed.

ABAYA

One afternoon, at a gathering with friends, from the corner of the living room I heard a friend of my mom's—she, too, Italian, married to a Saudi— ask my mother casually, in Italian, "Is Jasmin already a *young lady*?" I knew what that meant. I was appalled and offended that they were openly and comfortably discussing my personal business. My ears zoned in on their conversation and everything else around me was muted. I couldn't hear my friends giggling and talking, or the Italian music playing in the background through the VCR/TV, and I couldn't taste the tiramisù, which was a specialty treat prepared by this friend, who was not only a great cook but, now I realized, a nosy one, too.

The two of them exchanged no more than two sentences about the status of my womanhood. A question was asked, and my mom answered with a simple "not yet," and that was that.

I was agitated but had to contain it. I was furious but had to hide it. I was scared but had to brush it off.

The innocent and unburdened part of my girlhood would immediately be replaced with a black veil and the possibility of future grooms knocking at the door, exercising the art of arranged marriages that every girl, regardless of how beautiful, rich, or neither, would experience. In that moment, I decided that when that day came, when I became a "young lady," no one would know about it, and no one would talk about it. What seemed to be a natural and exciting time in a *young lady*'s life, was a horror in mine. My friends and cousins were beaming in anticipation, and I envied their conviction. Soon after girls began to menstruate, they started to picture their lives as wives and mothers, taking every step, in order to be seen, and *noticed* by vigilant mothers hunting for brides for their eligible bachelor sons.

A year later, I did, in fact, become a young lady, and as I did with all the promises I made, I kept this one, revealing nothing to anyone, not even my mother. I was eleven. I was tall and very thin. No signs of change appeared on my skinny boyish body. I was mortified at the sight of the first drop of blood in my underwear, which I threw in the trash, for fear of being discovered. Maybe because I was so young, my cycles were mild and my symptoms were non-existent, so getting through the monthly event was manageable. I used toilet paper to create thin pads that I could flush down the toilet. And I developed an effective method to wash my underwear in the bidet and then hide it in a corner of my closet to dry. At all costs, I wanted to postpone what I knew would happen when a girl reached puberty. She is expected to perform all religious practices including covering the hair with a *hijab,* and as is the case in more conservative countries like Saudi Arabia, a veil that covers the face, as well as the *abaya,* the cloak that covers a woman's body. All these clothing items are black, which made dealing with the heat of the desert climate almost unbearable, when by contrast, the men dressed in white *thobes* and *ghutras,* the white headdress.

The school I attended had a gate monitor who stood on the inside of the main gate and watched the girls each day as they entered and exited the school. Based on their physical appearance, and the development of their bodies (regardless of whether they had started menstruating or not yet) the monitor ordered the girls to show up at school the next day covered with an abaya and veil.

I dreaded going in and out of school every day because I feared being told, "It is time." I tried hard to hide behind my mother—who wore the abaya and veil—each time we passed through the gate of doom.

Like clockwork, my sister May became a young lady a year after I quietly went through the change myself. She was visibly curvier and more feminine than I was. Unlike me, she naturally and confidently announced it, even though she was surprised to have beat me to it. The next month, without hesitation, I also made the announcement at home, knowing that my con-cealment had run its course. This time-altered event remained a secret for decades.

Not long after May's menarche, the infamous gate monitor took one look at her as we left school and said, "Tomorrow you come to school in an abaya." May was devastated. We got in the car, and it seemed as though her world had come crashing down. I realized that May was excited about becom-ing a young woman but dreaded wearing the abaya. Perhaps the fact that I remained undeclared compounded her distress. It did seem unfair that May got called out before her older sister, and while I felt sad for her, I was glad for my temporary reprieve.

When we got home, my mother shared the news with my father: it was time to take May shopping for an abaya and veil. My dad—visibly not thrilled at the idea of his little girls becoming women quite so soon—said, "Jasmin will also need one."

"*What*?" I yelled, "*Why*? I was not told I needed one yet!"

"You are older, you cannot go around town uncovered when your younger sister is. What will people say?"

That's right. *What will people say*? This was my father, who didn't view the occasion as negotiable.

The abaya was a rite of passage for many young girls. It symbolized a new status, a small sense of importance in a society that didn't acknowledge our existence beyond the minimal assigned roles. We were an important collective, as long as we fulfilled our duties and met social standards with optimal enthusiasm. Individually, however, there was little room for growth and accomplishments.

This was the law, not only of the land, but of God since the constitution of Saudi Arabia is in fact the Koran. I resented it. I took it upon myself to find evidence in the holy book about this law which I triumphantly failed to do. There is no clear statement that women ought to be covered from head to toe. The interpretations of both the Koran and the Prophet Mohammad's sayings are many, depending on the scholars and their lineage. It appears the laws and rules were a right given to males, by males, and so it has remained for centuries.

I realized early on that questioning and challenging anything was a sure way to invite trouble. Many teachers scolded me for asking too many questions, and during a parent-teacher conference, when I was in ninth grade, my religion teacher told my mother I should stop asking so many questions and stop thinking about so many things. She advised my mother to encourage me to sit in the classroom quietly and learn the information given to us without debating and seeking answers to questions that have not been posed and should not be posed. When my mother came home and shared my teacher's frustration, she told me a story about her father, "When your Nonno was in seminary his teachers often scolded him for asking too many questions, and one of those teachers told him he could never be a priest because his questions went against the doctrine." That must have been the day my Nonno leaned into atheism. Like him, I too began to question this whole God thing and all the rules *He* imposed on us.

My teacher's comment, I knew, was a consequence to a question I had asked in class, "How is it logical that Beethoven was born with musical genius, if God said music is a sin? Isn't that a form of cruel torture?"

"These are not questions to ask. You cannot defy Allah's words. Just sit quietly and don't overthink this or try to debate it," replied the teacher with restrain and frustration.

"But...--" I tried to ask.

"Don't argue!" she demanded.

Since that day, I chose to be uninvolved in class. I escaped reality as I daydreamed about meeting Michael Jackson or being swept off my feet by Duran Duran's heartthrob bass player, John Taylor. I conjured up memories of my Italian summers and envisioned myself in a life that looked nothing like the one I was stuck in. Time in class became time to elude.

The school year dragged on since I became less engaged in class. I longed for the arrival of the summer vacation when I tasted upcoming freedom. As we boarded the international airline at the airport in Saudi Arabia,

I knew freedom lasted only a few weeks. As soon as the plane took off, most women shed the layer of abaya and veil, revealing modern top fashion outfits worthy of a Milano runway. There was a declaration in this behavior, a slight protest, a way to not only feel seen and heard, but also to be in control of our own lives—a boost to our sense of worthiness.

Our social behavior did not change much once we unveiled ourselves because most of us still struggled with the firm grip of the masculine mentality in our families. We were granted small freedoms, but we were still expected to abide by the code of conduct that was established and ingrained in our culture. We could not date, or develop a relationship with any male, even in friendship. Our dress code was to remain modest, and we were expected to stay within the confines of the family fence. No spontaneous teen adventure, or away-from-home trips with friends or at camp.

Nonetheless, during those days in Italy I let my imagination roam. I was determined to be optimistic, a notion that I gathered from my mom's book of optical illusions, which addressed the philosophy of the glass: half full or half empty? Seeing that our survival depended on our choices, I infused my half-filled Saudi glass, with Italian flower petals, flavors, and ice cubes, which made for a very impressive, delicious, beautiful, and full drink. This is how I survived.

Every little Italian adventure became an adventure of a lifetime, and I wasn't going to waste a moment of it. Going to restaurants with my family, especially a pizzeria, was a favorite summer pastime. "Prosciutto & funghi," pizza, with an orange San Pellegrino was my usual order. I joyously fed coins in the jukebox, selecting song after song while the grown-ups talked. I didn't want those nights to end. My dad drank Peroni beer and took a few bites of pizza, usually preferring a veal steak or "prosciutto & melone." My siblings and I sat at the end of the table, and I watched my father take sips of beer, interrupting a soft, resting smile that remained on his face most of the time that we were around my Italian relatives. He seemed relaxed, at ease, himself.

Wearing large hoop earrings, sporting her permed 'fro and glowing with sun-kissed bronze skin, my mom looked happy too. She had the help of our nanny to manage our needs and enjoyed the company of her family over a glass of wine and fine Italian antipasti. This was the life I wished I had every day. Each August when this sweet interlude ended, I had to dig my abaya out and have it ready to wrap me and hide me. Before landing in the Riyadh airport, I would express my sadness to my mother. I wanted her to say, "I know, me too." Instead, she responded, "It's special in Italy because everyone is on vacation and the weather is beautiful; you wouldn't love it as much when it's cold, rainy and everyone is at school."—Oh, but I would.

A DESERT OF CONTRADICTIONS

Riyadh was a new and modern city. I saw the buildings shoot up in the middle of the desert and witnessed monuments erected along with the growth of propaganda and patriotism. The capital was taking shape, and the desert was coming to life in an artificial, affluent, and contemporary way. People's lives were changing, and the exterior of those lives told stories that sparked pride and boasted prosperity. Even as the city grew on every economic level, personal growth and intellectual development remained taboo, this was a consequence of the continued conflict between cultural traditionalism and educational progressiveness. Many Saudi tribes adapted to the new way of life, but some chose to remain in the desert of their sacred land. These nomadic Bedouins were still a prominent collective in the region. They had travelled for centuries upon centuries across the sands. I experienced an occasional taste of this life when my uncles would pitch desert tents for overnight camping and prepared *Mandi,* meat cooked in an underground pit. It was an existence that celebrated sustainability and heritage. This way of life had become a recreational sport, and only a handful of clans continued to live this way. Political, religious, and social constructs stripped away their tribal freedom and replaced it with sovereign governance. Eventually, I was stunned to learn of the many similarities between the indigenous people of America and Arabia, a reminder of the beauty most cultures share, free from colonialism and imperialism, at the core of their natural and authentic existence.

Although I was fascinated by the past, I was born into this modern Arabian renaissance. The modernization was so fast paced that I witnessed infrastructural transformations, from commercial development to domestic architecture. We visited friends who were moving into new homes that showcased their westernized attitudes and new-found wealth: giant villas with pools and fountains; marble countertops and floors; European chandeliers hanging in several rooms; dining tables that could seat up to twenty; and multiple sitting rooms to accommodate different occasions or gender segregation. These houses made our six-bedroom, three living room, seven-bathroom home with a pool, seem modest. My parents were not seduced by these external riches and made certain neither were we.

In the evenings after dinner, in front of the TV, my siblings and I lounged on the ground with our heads propped against the traditional floor furniture that was in our Arabic living room.

"Ella, can you bring me a glass of water?" I would plead loudly.

"Come here and get it yourself, please!" my mom would call out from the kitchen. Not knowing she was within earshot; I was embarrassed to be called out. My mom had no tolerance for entitled behavior.

"Pick up the mess in the living room!" she would say before she went to bed. She didn't need to point at all the pillows out of place and the explosion of snacks on the floor.

This messaging was confusing because we were pampered in many ways—my bed was always made when I came home from school, and the house was cleaned daily with all meals prepared and served—I barely learned how to cook or do the laundry, nonetheless my mother taught us other ways to be responsible. If she needed help, she asked one of us, not the maids, because the servants in our house were performing a job that we were not allowed to interrupt. Perhaps it was in how my parents raised us and educated us, or perhaps it was in seeing how the rest of the world lived, but my brief sense of entitlement came from a place of insecurity and cultural pressure. I saw those who had more and those who had less. The facade of grand living around me was obvious, and my need to belong to something more real was also a formidable part of my awareness.

Few people outside of the Kingdom understood or imagined what was happening to this land, which was only ever described for Westerners in fairy tales and folklore. Visions of Bedouins riding horses and camels, women veiled and discreetly tucked inside of desert tents with children around them—these were the scenes depicted in old films and popular culture. In more contemporary times, Westerners daftly imagined a barbaric society suddenly rich from oil, nomadically living the desert life with strange habits and practices, to today's media hype where sadly the labels of Islamic terrorist and Arab have become synonymous. During our trips to Italy, we were often asked if we rode to school on camels and if we had barrels of "petrol" in our backyard. We rarely enlightened them with the reality taking shape in our country and instead played along, making up stories of our camels and tent bedrooms, just to see the reactions of our listeners and, later, laugh at their ignorance.

My parents built their first and only home during the early 1970's in what became the heart of Riyadh. My mother, who sold her property in Florence, Italy, chose to use her financial profits to build a modern and spacious home in the outskirts of the rapidly growing city. Around them, only two other homes existed, and the streets were unpaved. A few miles away, the Riyadh airport —which eventually became the military airport when the state-of-the-art King Khalid International Airport was built in the mid 1980's—stood as a reminder that life in Riyadh was not as secluded and isolated as the rest of the world thought.

The hospital where I was born was the largest and most prestigious medical facility of the time, now a clinic that serves low-income patients and traditional families, was also in the neighborhood. Not far from our house was the main local "souk," an outdoor market. Jewelry stores, which sold mainly Saudi gold, were blinding galleries of shimmer and shine. Traditional Saudi jewelry pieces, including full chest armor style necklaces, hung on the walls of the stores with no concern about robbery and targeted theft. The sense of safety and honor was at the core of how merchants and businesses worked. The jewelry sold was only for women because, aside from the occasional ring or watch, men do not wear jewelry. These stores were a spectacle of gold and black, from the wall-to-wall display to the head-to-toe abaya-covered bodies that flocked to these shiny showrooms.

My mother, who sewed her own dresses in the early years, shopped for fabrics at the souk. Eventually, when my sister and I needed formalwear, we frequented a custom tailoring workshop, where we would spend an entire afternoon being measured for our seasonal dresses. My father took my brother to have their summer and winter *thobes* custom-tailored as well. We never paid full price for anything at the souk because bargaining was half the experience. Not only do Arabs haggle but so do the Italians, and when I eventually travelled to the U.S. I was eager to show-off my sophisticated negotiation skills but was met with odd and indignant reactions when I asked for a discount at the Gap.

One store we often visited was *Al-Mutanabbi*. My mom liked to remind me, "In the early seventies this store was a hole in the wall with a few basic self-care products, nothing like the fancy emporium it is today." We filled our basket with make-up, hair products, beauty care items, perfumes, household gadgets, and new fashion trends. The two other stores I loved to visit were *Jareer* Bookstores, and *Ahmed Jamal* Toy Store. I inherited my love for books and art supplies from both my parents. As soon as I walked into the book-store, the smell of paper transported me to a happy place, an experience that persists into the present. The toy store was stocked with stuffed animals—a veritable "Toy Story"—that came to life in my presence. For my 6th birthday, my mother gave me a life size Pekinese dog, Peki, my pet, who I never thought of as a toy.

My mother and my culture were always present to remind me that animals belonged outside, in their natural habitat. This prohibition prompted me to rely on my imagination, especially during my summers in Italy. At a corner souvenir store in Rome, I bought a plastic turtle that fit in the palm of my eight-year-old hand. I fed it crumbs from my sandwich and bathed it in the sink of the hotel room. I cuddled it under my neck when I went to sleep, and in the morning tied a thin thread around its neck because it needed a leash if I were to take it out for a walk. I loved all animals, but more than anything I could wish for, what I really wanted was a pet dog. I knew it was never going to happen. I watched people freely walk their dogs on leashes in the streets of Europe. It looked like the most amazing thing to experience. I saw them play fetch and rub their dog's ears while the collars jingled. I understood the dog's body language as if it were instinctively my own. The tail wag, the floppy tongue, the fidgety dance, and the attentive eyes. These were signs of joy and love, and I desperately wanted to have that unconditional friendship in my life. My turtle's thread leash eventually turned into an invisible leather and chain leash when I upgraded my plastic pet turtle to a full size, lively, invisible German Shepard named "Cucciolo" (Koo-Cho-lo, Italian for puppy).

In Riyadh I found comfort in the bookstore as I searched for dog breed encyclopedias, and the toy stores that sold stuffed animals. As the years went by and my interests expanded beyond books and stuffed animals, I remember finding Michael Jackson T. Shirts and his well-known Thriller jacket sold secretly at the *Al-Mutanabbi* store. These locally-owned stores in Riyadh remained in business over the years, but their clientele changed as the city progressed.

In the mid-80s the mall craze landed in the heart of the desert, planting deep roots like a thirsty resilient acacia tree. The phenomenon of department stores, brand names, and indoor shopping was clearly here to stay, and no better place in the world where this model could be more appealing—away from the outdoor heat, strolling in air-conditioned marble buildings, observing, on headless mannequins, the latest fashion trends from Europe and America, and joyfully living on the materialistic gains of this newfound progress. The contradictions were unmistakable, but the lure was so charming that men and women of all socio-economic and cultural backgrounds saw themselves drawn to this unusual and unnatural new experience.

During the day, most stores were open, closing five times between dawn and sunset for prayer. Expatriates and western wives, like my mom, were the usual daytime shoppers. As the sun set, when the imam called the last prayer, the city came to life. At night the heat subsided and with the long break between the last prayer call of the evening and the next call at dawn, it was convenient to experience an active consumeristic nocturnal social life. Riyadh looked like Las Vegas at night—excluding the casinos, strippers and shows—tall buildings standing proudly in the desert, telling a story of cultural accomplishment and prosperity. The blinding lights that blinked and glowed in every color hypnotized the inhabitants of this ancient and sacred land. The nighttime city scene resembled Hollywood movies, but entertainment, socialization, and liberalism were unwelcome hidden side effects of this rapid change. Today Saudi Arabia boasts a different story, one that hangs on a thread between total progress and a tit for tat progress.

The government sought the assistance of the Religious Police, known as *Mutawa* (official title in English: Committee for the Promotion of Virtue and the Prevention of Vice) to enforce Islamic values and uphold the strictest form of segregation and anti-corruption values. They made sure stores remained closed during prayer times, but their focus was on women's conduct in public. A stroll in any modern district, where young women and young men flocked, was monitored by the *Mutawa*, chasing off young men from areas heavily trafficked by young girls, but focusing their unwavering energies on women, of all ages and all origins—enforcing their laws.

What's remarkable is that no mention of their codes of conduct for Saudi women are found in any Islamic scripture—demanding they cover, not only their bodies and hair, but their faces, and their hands, imposing their silence. According to their ideology, the female voice is one of the strongest sexual temptations for men. Because of these unwavering rules, women were harassed relentlessly, especially if they were seen shopping without a male guardian. "Cover up woman!" was their signature command, as they waved a cane, everywhere we encountered them in public.

In the midst of modern buildings and luxurious palaces, conservative reminders remained visible on almost every block. The neighborhood Mosques could be heard at each prayer call. The minaret transmitted the amplified voice of the mosques' imam during prayer calls and during post-prayer sermons. When I was a very young child, I thought the minaret was "Allah" because that's the only word I understood coming out of it. It scared me, and since there was a mosque and minaret in every corner of every street, I felt watched by God all the time, judged, and punished if I ever strayed from his rules.

As I grew older, I developed a minaret trauma. I heard the angry male voices coming out of it through full-volume microphones for all to hear, even in the privacy of their homes, "Destroy the Jews and the infidels! We are all doomed to hell unless we follow Allah's word! Say NO to Satan!" The message condemned corruption from the West and hyped the Islamic nation to fight any threat and save the holy lands.

The clash of so many odd realities created a hostile, confused, and agitated environment for many young Saudis. I know it did for me. We stepped into an artificial world of modernity and progress while dressed in medieval costumes that cloaked our jeans and T-shirts. I craved to establish my sense of style and to individuate my identity. With everyone dressed—covered—in black, I had no way to assert my sense of self. I made it a point to wear *my* clothes under the abaya, even under my school uniform. My ripped stone-washed jeans and my Duran Duran T-shirts enforced my inner freedom. I wore mis-matched socks on purpose and tied a bandanna around my thigh like Punky Brewster did. I covered my denim jacket in button pins that not only had faces of my favorite musicians, but also affirmed statements like "end all wars," "peace," "freedom," "love not hate," "save the earth," "music is my life," and Lennon's message "imagine."

The contradictions tormented me. Italy was my sanctuary, until one summer when my father, who remained in Riyadh for work, remodeled the bedrooms into a modern and highly efficient retreat for teenage girls. We had our own full bathroom, a bonus room, which I turned into my studio lounge, a Hollywood style vanity with mirror and lights, which May turned into her personal spa, custom-built beds with shelves, and floor-to-ceiling closets. I had a new safe place in which I could be myself.

Within days, May and I covered what little wall space we had left with posters. Michael Jackson, Duran Duran, Wham!, Bruce Springsteen, Madonna, Whitney Houston, and several Italian heartthrobs including Eros Ramazzotti, Edoardo Bennato, and Luis Miguel, all greeted us each morning when we woke up. May had a small boombox, and I had a large stereo with speakers. Sometimes we fought about it, and sometimes we diplomatically discussed a fair schedule for playing music. She enjoyed most of the music I played, but I had to tolerate Madonna, Belinda Carlisle, and—the British topless model turned singer—Samantha Fox.

May admired women, idolized some of the biggest sex symbols of the century, but I was drawn to androgynous artists and fashioned my own style after them. My sister was more secure in her gender and femininity, as well as in her role as a girl and then woman in the world, and because of that she never identified as a staunch feminist. I felt strongly about gender injustices and openly labeled myself as hardcore feminist. I was boy crazy, man crazy, but also irate, disgusted, and angry about patriarchy and misogyny. This amplified the contradictions I was struggling with. I chose to be less feminine because I was turned off by the stereotypes of womanhood, especially in a country where womanhood is monolithic. I didn't spend a lot of time in front of the closet, making up my mind. When I was not in my school uniform, I usually wore jeans, a baggy hoodie and styled my long mullet by blow-drying my bangs into a wave. Meanwhile, May would ask me, "Do I look fat?" as she posed in her shoulder padded orange sweater and striped skirt. She sat in front of the mirror and, like the artist she is, decorated her face with the multi-color palette of make-up. "No, you're fine," I would respond, feeling uninterested in her excessively girlie ritual. I often teased her, "If anyone can't find you, they should look for the nearest mirror, chances are you fell asleep in front of it!" When it came to style, she drew inspiration from Marilyn Monroe and Madonna; instead, I revered Michael Jackson, Duran Duran, Spandau Ballet, David Bowie, Queen, Culture Club, Alice Cooper, and many other bands that displayed a blunt gender-bending sense of expression, until after my teens when my bohemian inner-hippie stabilized my sense of fashion once and for all.

The bedroom that my father designed for us replaced Banga as it became my stage, my forest, my club, my playground—any location that suited my dreams. I spent hours performing in front of an imaginary audience. I sang Debbie Gibson hits—which were relatable, given that Debbie and I were about the same age. I also composed music on my keyboard and recorded my (unreleased) debut album "Surface of Illusion" on cassette. To accomplish this, I used my impressive—by impressive I mean, I had to put this thing together all by myself, using my ingenuity to cobble together the tech gear—state of the art stereo, cables, mics, headphones, and electronic instruments.

But usually, I danced. I closed the door to the contradicting reality I faced every day and recreated Michael Jackson videos or choreographed my own. Spinning barefoot on the carpet and moonwalking across the length of the room, I entered another realm. There, I was blinded by the stage lights that were in my head. I was overwhelmed by the applause I heard in my head. Through dance, I embodied the emotions that lived in my head.

When I left my bedroom, I concealed my ambitions without abandoning my thoughts and feelings, because I couldn't imagine being without them. But I covered my artistic expression with a thin cape, for safekeeping. Even though my family was privy to my love for dance and performance, I withheld aspects of what seemed like an enchanter's performance. They couldn't see it all. When I left the house, the abaya cloaked me against my will, and the only way I could make peace with it was to view it as a magician's prop. I became increasingly adept at manipulation, slight-of-hand, smoke and mirrors—the illusions that I crafted—that slowly and artfully became my inner truth, regardless of what visible image I projected.

At every age, in every situation, I was swiftly sorting through my mental bag of tricks, to present the false impression or forge the convincing gimmick in order to endure the surreal and overwhelming surroundings that became more hypnagogic as I became more aware. This felt like a game; I was balancing the cultural contradictions with my own self-realization to survive. It wasn't until recently, when I became more involved in activism work and learned first-hand from marginalized groups, that what I went through is known as passing or assimilation. When I spoke Arabic I forced a local dialect, convincing conservative and traditional individuals whom I encountered, that I was a legitimate Saudi. I went from being a little girl who barely spoke Arabic to a preteen who used her talents as an impersonator to talk like everyone around her to fit in.

Day in and day out, we implemented the same ritualistic protocol, summoning the driver to take us from point A to point B. Having no privacy or control over where I went, and how long I stayed. As I grew older, I became increasingly vexed by customs and protocols that seems humiliating and demeaning. Most women enjoyed the privilege and luxury of having such service. The driver was not only an employee, but to many, he was a possession. I marveled in utter discomfort and disapproval, as I watched how some women talked to their drivers, ordering them around without curtesy words like "please" and "thank you," never making eye contact or relating to them as people. Our family, by contrast, became very connected with the employees in our home. I could not imagine asking for services they were paid to perform without being courteous and respectful. I apologized if the driver waited too long, and I calculated my own errands with his other duties, such as grocery shopping, garden maintenance, and housekeeping. In my mind, they were part of the family.

As their employer and sponsor, my father was legally liable for their conduct. On occasion, we encountered some troubling behaviors. The first was our driver, Mel, Ella's husband, who was lured into an illegal gambling ring, making him disappear at all hours of the day and night. Often, Mel was not home at 7 am when he was supposed to take us to school. This disruption imposed the driving duties on my father, which of course, my mother could not do. But perhaps the most troubling event was that of Freddy and Eva's arrest. Freddy and Eva, a couple from the Philippines, worked as driver and nanny in our home for several years. They were caught and jailed for months before being sent back to their home in Manila after a horrific punishment of lashes and the outcome of being barred from reentering The Kingdom.

Freddy and Eva had run afoul of the country's conservative Islamic practices, which were not only the way of life but also law, with the rigid expectations imposed on both Saudis and non-Saudis, alike. Foreigners entering the country receive a list—and if lucky, a training—on how to avoid a harsh and even fatal consequence. Murder, drugs, alcohol, gambling, prostitution, homosexuality, theft, and immodesty are only some of the major offenses listed. Such laws made life fairly safe, but also opened a way for a lucrative underground market. Freddy and Eva were both educated and bright individuals. Sadly, working as professionals in their own country yielded a third of the income they made in the Middle East as hired help. While this arrangement was often enough for servants, it was not for Freddy and Eva.

One afternoon while I was doing homework, the phone rang and a rude male voice demanded to speak to Abdulaziz, my father.

"Who is this?" I asked, with an equally rude tone.

"This is al-*Hai-a'a*," he replied.

I ran to find my father and told him who was on the line.

He was shaken and immediately picked up the phone, "Yes sir, sure sir, yes, I'll be right there." My father took off, and all he said was, "*They* arrested Freddy and Eva around the corner."

"They" was the al-*Hai-a'a*, the abbreviated name for The Committee for the Promotion of Virtue and the Prevention of Vice, the organization for which the *Mutawas* worked. The religious police had arrested our driver and maid, and I was the only one in the family who was not surprised.

Prior to her arrest, Eva had worked for us as a nanny. She was a young attractive single gal who spoke fluent English and who evinced a youthful and Americanized attitude. I was a teenager at the time, and barely younger than her. We had become friends, and enjoyed talking about music, movies, fashion, and culture. Eva traveled with us to Italy while her older sister, Lidia, who was our head housekeeper, and Lidia's husband, Nestor, who was our driver, took care of the house during our months of absence. Eva and her fiancé replaced Lidia and Nestor when they ended their years of service in our home and returned to the Philippines to be with their children. Eva also enlisted her cousin, Maricel, as the second maid and nanny. The arrangement couldn't be more pleasing to my parents, who, by now, were about to hire the third couple from the same family, starting with Ella and Mel over a decade earlier.

After Eva and Freddy got married, they came to work for us. From the first time I met Freddy, I felt a powerful uneasiness. Something about him made me uncomfortable, almost on edge. He was an arrogant and conceited man. I had many confrontations with him, but my parents begged me to be polite and not cause trouble because losing him would create the inconvenience of finding and hiring a new couple.

When we had some remodeling done to the house, the carpet removed from our formal living room remained in good condition. My father arranged for it to be given to a charity. The night before it was to be picked up, while everyone at home was asleep, I was up late studying for a final. It was 2 am, and I heard noises coming from outside. I looked out my bedroom window, which was above the main entrance to our home, and saw a gathering of men whispering around where the old carpet lay in several large rolls. I saw Freddy engaging three or four other men who, with efficiency, took the rolls of carpet as they handed Freddy cash. Stunned, I told my parents the next day, but they chose to let it go, only making it easier for him to continue his shady and dishonest schemes.

Minutes after my father ran out the door following the phone call about Freddy and Eva's arrest, I watched out the window as he returned with the police, who escorted Freddy and Eva in hand and ankle cuffs. They made their way to the couple's bedroom where they turned it upside down, going through all their personal belongings. In their room, we found stolen items from our home: jewelry, expensive gadgets, trinkets, and more, all worth hundreds of rials, things that we knew were missing, but thought had been misplaced.

We found out that Freddy and Eva had been under surveillance for several months. They had been making and selling alcohol in and from our home. They carried it in the back of the car to deliver to customers, while driving us around. In the glove compartment, we found thousands of rials. The distillery was in their room, and the hiding spot was the sewer of our home.

The adolescent in me felt vindicated. They had a lucrative business, one that by local standards was both sinful and illegal. I knew Freddy was the brains behind it. When he came to work for us, I not only struggled with his sexist and disrespectful attitude, but also lost a friend. Eva had turned on the family and adopted his distant and boorish behavior. Freddy corrupted his wife and endangered my family, and I had no ounce of empathy for him.

That evening he called the house, "Jasmin, tell sir to bring me clean towels when he comes to see us tonight at the jail."

Sir was my father, and Freddy's demand made me wonder if I misheard.

"Say that again, Freddy," I said in a perplexed tone.

"They only give us one towel, I need more," he replied, as if he was an entitled customer at the Hilton.

"Fuck you, Freddy!" I said before hanging up the phone. I disconnected it, so that his attempt to call back would go unanswered. I knew my kind-hearted father would probably oblige him, but the angry teen in me felt like justice was finally served, and I intended to keep it that way.

The contradictions in the world in which I lived penetrated my psyche. I was not sure how I felt about the punishments enforced by the government on governed. I was caught between my personal views on morality—I did not feel strongly about Freddy and Eva making and selling alcohol—and the righteous morality that was imposed upon me against my will. Although I refused to feel victimized by these societal codes, I also did not recognize that my subconscious frustrations had turned into resentment toward others. Freddy was a vile and cunning man; he got what he deserved. But my jubilation in the aftermath was more an indication of my pain than it was of justice being served.

Maricel continued to work for us, and we hired a local driver as a temporary arrangement. Everything continued as it had before. We were not debilitated by the absence of Freddy and Eva, and life went on in all its predictable ways. I still summoned the driver when I needed to go anywhere, and the mundane experiences of occasional outings continued to plague my constant unfulfilled thoughts.

Sitting in the back of the car, looking out the window at the six lane streets and highways, driving for hours from one side of town to the other, fighting traffic and chaos, observing the never ending construction of new sky-scrapers and national monuments, billboards advertising Chanel products and Louis Vuitton handbags, I witnessed change from behind the windshield, a world where only men were visible in the street while women remained invisible, driven around for essential purposes only: school, work, shopping, hospital or social visits.

The change was constant and material, with no sign of social and intellectual advances, and still today, these changes continue to impress the global community and economic competitors, while any attempt to seek true freedom and liberation, or democracy and justice is met with punishment and demise.

I watched and observed this unbelievable life of oppression and control as the driving force of all conduct, where a 1400-year-old religion was used to establish the laws of the land, and where society was ruled by shame and strict morality. I tried to set aside the growing urgency of experiencing cerebral incitement and personal fulfillment in a world where I could simply walk to the park with a dog on the leash, unveiled and free to speak my mind.

TEACHER

Mrs. Boissel was like no other teacher. From the first time she set foot in the classroom, she took command, like an iron-handed sea captain. Unlike the overcrowded public schools, the private schools in Saudi Arabia limited the number of students in each class. We spent the academic year with the same group of 20 students who shared a homeroom teacher. The exception to this was English class, where girls were grouped based on their language skills into four classes formed by the level of fluency in the English language: group A always had fluent students with a native speaking teacher (British, American, Irish, Canadian ...etc.); in group B—the class type that my mom taught—the students were very comfortable with English as a second language and the teacher spoke like a native, although not always native herself; in group C the students had a very limited and modest grasp on the language and the teacher was a native Arab with a degree in English; and finally, in group D, the students had little to no background in the English language, and like in group C, had a native Arab teacher.

In my English class, I felt at ease and authentic because I was with my real friends, almost all of them half western like myself, or with lived experiences in the west, and because we were guided by women I felt culturally very close to. Each fall, we waited in anticipation to see if there were any girls upgraded to our group from the previous year, or perhaps a new student from a bi-cultural family who had a solid foundation in English. In group A, our English teachers were expatriates, which meant that we had a new one every other year or so. We were always excited to find out what accent we'd be mimicking behind her back, and what cultural quirks we'd be exposed to from her native land.

On the first day of school of junior high, a petite woman with red hair entered the classroom, commanding our attention and respect without making much eye contact with any of us. She was stern and acrimonious, qualities that were amplified in the military march that she put on display through her relentless pacing. She introduced herself and got right to business. We were stunned and unimpressed. Day one was done, and none of us responded well to her. The classroom felt like a balloon that had been punctured without warning.

I went home and told my mom "Captain Von Trapp is our new English teacher; all she needs is a whistle!" I was concerned about having her as my teacher—so much so that I considered dropping down to group B, where I would be with less fluent girls but safely beyond the reach of this formidable teacher.

She didn't smile much. She wasn't impressed about the fact that we spoke English well; she didn't pay us compliments and didn't cut us any slack. Each hour she spent in the classroom with us that first week, she talked. Mrs. Boissel talked about world politics, she talked about Gabon where she taught before coming to Saudi Arabia, she talked about Ireland where she was from, she talked about France where her husband was from. She talked about all the things she had done and places she had been, but we didn't get to talk— hardly at all.

She informed us, "Your homework for next week is to write an essay about someone you like and admire. Tell me a little about their life, the work they did, but mostly why you chose them and what their work means to you."

Yes, Mrs. Boissel gave us homework the first week of school. Who does that? I now look back at the indignant reaction we all had and am shocked by my sense of privilege.

I wrote an essay about Beethoven because I was inspired by his music and his determination in the face of his deafness and financial woes. He awed me because he composed his incomparable 5th symphony after he lost his hearing. In my essay, I easily described why and how Beethoven came to be one of my heroes, and how it was possible for me to forgive his unkindness, which I understood resulted from the unjust torment he faced with his disability. I made excuses for him and justified his behavior—he was a troubled genius after all—as I imagined him living with the wicked trick fate played on him. He had no say. No control.

I was proud of that essay, and even prouder when I got an "A."

To my surprise, the work for that essay wasn't quite done. Mrs Boissel called the class to attention, looked directly at me, and asked, "How do you think Saudi women can be heard in the rest of the world where, due to their culture, their voices are deemed non-existent? When Beethoven found the ability to create music he couldn't hear, where do you think he found the perseverance? Do you think Arab and Saudi women can find ways to voice their ideas? because no doubt they have many!" Mrs. Boissel continued looking at me and waited for an answer. I was caught off guard; how did she know I was interested in this topic?

It became clear to me why she began closing the door when she walked into the classroom each day. Besides my mother, I had never talked about such daring and rebellious topics with anyone else. Mrs. Boissel was interested, though. She had found the safest way to invite herself into our mental home. She got to know each one of us. She was not merely interested in the things I'd done and places I'd been, she was interested in far more than that.

The weekly homework essays became the most anticipated project of the weekend. I had never written essays in English before. The extent of my work had been practicing grammar and spelling by crafting paragraphs about my country, or about fictional scenarios. Mrs. Boissel opened my eyes and rattled my brain. For an hour a day, I forgot the harsh reality of my socially deprived life in Saudi Arabia. In her class I felt safe, excited, awake, and eager to participate.

Mrs. Boissel was worldly. She had lived in many places and shared many stories with us. She brought to life her former students, who existed in a far-away world, a world that lured my imagination. Every week Mrs. Boissel had us time-travel to the past and future using the topics she lectured on as our vessel. It was easy to be seated at my desk and feel like I was on a ship sailing the Atlantic Ocean as she shared historic facts of European immigrants sailing to the United States, or by contrast, landing in a modern airport on the east coast of the United States, to walk across a concrete jungle of modern buildings and monuments. I found myself in Africa, visiting with locals while I made my way around tiny villages on foot. At times her stories placed me on the back of a donkey, meeting folks in South America and exploring the ancient lands of past civilizations.

Each day, our vessel changed in Mrs. Boissel's class, and I became an intellectual explorer, guided by this phenomenally educated adventurer. She followed up these journeys by inviting us to discuss and debate—by now, her smile was a predictable gesture each time one of us lit up and started an answer with, "well, I think…," yes, we were "thinking," and nothing gave her more joy; her mission was accomplished.

We were encouraged to deconstruct modern political models, as well as to question standard practices in mainstream corporations, global organizations, societal norms, and cultural barriers. There were days when I gleefully wondered if what happened in our English classroom might get us in trouble. Taboo topics and women thinkers were a dangerous combination in a place where our role, both at school and in society, was to be proper women with just enough education to raise our national standing in the world, and to serve the community in limited fields that abided by our religious values. Women were unheard and our intellectual contributions were not welcome and certainly not encouraged. I knew this. Every girl knows this from the moment thoughts are formed. This was the society that I grew up in. Over time, changes have happened, but they were not fast enough for me to blossom in every pressing and productive way.

In my two years with Mrs. Boissel, I wrote about the construct of higher education, researched the American Civil War, and explored how drugs in the 1980's were becoming an out-in-the-open epidemic. We discussed the 1988 U.S. presidential election and debated the pros-and-cons of the candidates, Bush and Dukakis—a debate staged with a mock election—a democratic process that was unthought of and contradicted the constitutional ruling of the Saudi region. I read a biography of Michael Jackson in Italian and translated it into a book report in English. I wrote a paper on my visit to the Italian poet and writer Gabriele D'Annunzio's villa and adjunct library museum in Italy which, thanks to his eccentricities, was unlike any other national monument I'd seen.

We were invited to write poems, to articulate our passions and dreams as well as our worries and frustrations. She was thoughtful in how she empowered us. She somehow knew how to be respectful of the culture and its norms without provoking rebellious thinkers, while also staying deeply empathetic and compassionate toward each of her students. She was an activist just by showing up. Over the years while she was in Saudi Arabia, we occasionally socialized outside of school, and I met her daughters, who were around my age. My mother befriended her colleagues, and became a gracious host, bridging the western and local worlds together in our private home gatherings. Mrs. Boissel was able to talk about the mundane things and was concerned with topics beyond past tense verbs and sentence structure. Seeing Mrs. Boissel as a mother—with daughters I had more in common with than I would have imagined—broke down any dramatic impressions I still held about her. She showed me that a woman can be all things.

Before turning fifteen, I talked about my upcoming birthday nonstop. Fifteen seemed auspicious. Mrs. Boissel and her daughters were among the guests at my birthday party.

"Happy Birthday!" She said in her cheerful voice as she handed me a box with the name of one of my favorite local bakeries on it.

"Whoa!" I exclaimed when I opened the box. I felt goosebumps all over my body. The beautiful cake was inscribed in frosting with, "Jasmin, 15 AT LAST!"

It was one of my all-time favorite gifts. She didn't need to say much. I looked into her beautiful green eyes and observed her earnest smile that was unique to this intimate moment. The statement on the cake told me that she was paying attention to what was important to me—to my adolescent need to be seen as a person.

I cannot imagine my life today without the permanent imprint of Mary Boissel's influence. I have learned to trust the intuitive part of myself, which was in some measure fed, stimulated, agitated, shaken, and harvested by the teachings of this magnificent woman. She showed up when I needed it most. With one foot in adolescence and the other in adulthood, I was thrust into the prospect of becoming a strong and confident woman myself, even when the surroundings told me I was unworthy.

I pouted and protested every time my brother got to do things I couldn't do because he was a boy, and I was a girl. It felt unfair and cruel. My protests were futile at home and beyond. Yet my time with Mrs. Boissel unexpectedly introduced me to the true meaning and effective achievement of feminism and equality. On the surface it wasn't apparent, but deep in my subconscious she was a force that laid the foundation for my eventual understanding of what and how feminism works, and what today helps me navigate my frequent outbursts about injustice and inequality.

PART TWO:

THE CONTRIVANCE

ENDINGS

In high school, girls start thinking about their future. Not an unusual or uncommon thing for most young women around the world, except, back in those days, most girls around me were thinking of a future with a husband and family. This fantasyland was the peak time in a girl's life; to be seen and noticed by a prowling future-groom's mother was top priority. Often playing a game of fox and hound at various gatherings—such as weddings, parties, and even funerals— young girls wore their Sunday best to these events, and mothers solicited information about potential brides for their sons from the elders or well-known community gossips.

By their junior or senior years, many of my friends had already been matched in an arrangement. Soon after that, they became officially engaged and began planning a post-high-school-graduation wedding, while I was still trying to make sense of my purpose, either facing reality and accepting the fate that was clearly engraved for me or continuing to daydream of a seemingly impossible life of my choosing.

The incessant thoughts of my summer adventures in Italy kept me going until the next trip: crushes on cute guys, going to museums and parks, days at the beach and nights at the pizzeria with my family, weekends at the farm, magazine and cassette shopping with my friends downtown, and TV viewing with my grandmother in the evening. We brought home mental souvenirs but also video cassettes that we recorded in Italy of TV shows and music videos. These recordings that I played over and over, as well as the photo albums that I flipped through, and the long-distance letters I anticipated from my friends and relatives, were all tokens that kept me anchored in a world I only belonged to in theory.

My mother knew I struggled with a desperate yearning for another life and so she worked hard at seizing any opportunity that would offer us a cultural and social experience in Riyadh, like quietly going to the Italian, American, or German embassies for classical concerts of world-class chamber music acts and renowned soloists. As I held my breath and watched the musicians play, I longed for a personalized connection with them and dressed for the occasion. After one particularly unforgettable concert of classical Spanish music, in my velvet calf-length green skirt and white blouse, matching green eyeshadow and pink lip-gloss, I felt personally serenaded by the handsome Canadian soloist. I assertively asked the ushers for permission to meet him and collect an autograph.

"The concert was wonderful, thank you so much! Can I please have your autograph?" I asked in hopes of engaging in a longer conversation.

"Thank you! What's your name, sweetheart?" asked Chris, the flirty musician.

"Jasmin," I said bashfully.

"Jasmin, what a beautiful name! Are you a musician?" he asked with a grin.

"Yeah, kinda, I'm an amateur," I answered.

"Don't stop playing!" he said with a wink, handing me the autographed photo.

I walked away squealing as I read his note, *Jasmin! Thanks for coming out cutie! Love, Chris*

I often succeeded at creating a warm and meaningful encounter, perhaps not so much for them, but certainly for myself. I knew they would never remember me, but in the moments when we talked, it mattered that I was seen and valued by them. For just a few minutes, I felt like I was in touch with something that was so much a part of who I was. I belonged to another world, their world. I felt left behind when they left the stage and held on to the fantasy that penetrated my every contemplation.

One summer in Italy, my cousin Vince took me, my sister May, and our cousins Sabrina and Paola to what was essentially my first rock concert. It was Antonello Venditti, the Italian Eric Clapton. Up until that point, I only knew him by name. I was too young to be a fan of his music, which burst on the scene in the 1970's. At his concert I fell madly in love with him. His songs were powerful, his musical genius was distinct, and the crowd of his devoted fans inspired me. At the end of the concert, I heard one of the fans mention the name of the hotel where Antonello was staying. It was midnight, but I begged Vince to take us there. Vince has always had a soft spot for me, but that night I tested him, he was tired, and since he was not the star-struck type, he resisted. My persistence, however, was stronger. We arrived at the Hotel Kiris where a group of fans chanted Antonello's name and sang his songs. He waved from his balcony, and like a flash, faded into the curtains of his hotel suite. The fans expressed their love one more time before they, too, vanished into their cars and left.

Vince looked at me and said, "Ok, are you happy?"

"NO! I have to meet him!" I said assertively.

I made my way to the hotel entrance, which was closed and guarded by hotel security. I explained to them that *I was Antonello's biggest fan, that I had come all the way from Saudi Arabia to see him, and that for me, this was a pilgrimage; I had to meet him, or I would die.*

"Saudi Arabia? A likely story! More like Florence!"

Evidently, my mom's Tuscan accent had rubbed off on me, and I could not pretend to be a poor desperate tourist from a faraway land. I dug in my heels. I had to see Antonello! By now, Vince, May, and our cousins were yawning and sighing. It was 1 am, and they were ready to call it a night. The hotel staff felt the same, so one of the doormen decided to go inside and investigate the possibility of making my dream come true, or perhaps investigate the humane way to get rid of the pesky fan.

He finally came back and said, "Okay, so, Antonello is already in his robe and not in any shape to meet anyone, but he's willing to talk to you on the phone, if you will follow me to the lobby."

My group of relatives, suddenly alert, bounced in enthusiasm begging to follow me in, but the doorman said, "AH! No, not everyone, just the crazy one!"

I was the crazy one! I followed him to the lobby and spoke to the one and only Antonello Venditti, an artist who, up until that night, I hadn't known anything about, but who quickly became one of my all-time favorite singers.

Even now that it's been over thirty years since those days of secret planning and silent jubilation, I never take for granted going to a concert or attending a live performance. One of the most thrilling experiences of my life has been connecting with artists, which today I share with my musician sons. These childhood concerts are where I learned to appreciate the small things. Only much later in life did I realize that appreciating the small things, like children do, is the foundation for true happiness.

When I was consumed with frustration about the bigger picture of my oppressed existence, I was often comforted by the song lyrics that told stories of the underdog, by daydreaming of a different script, and by dancing in the spotlight for my invisible audience, the best audience in the world. I learned the important lesson of making the most of everything and making everything count.

In my secluded Saudi bubble, my experiences ranged from those intimate private concerts, to dancing and composing music in my room. Over the years this bubble included my *halfie* friends and weekly visits with my Saudi relatives. But being chased and harassed by the *Mutawa*, while being fed propaganda and distorted religion in school was the needle that constantly threatened the integrity of my bubble.

As time went by, however, some things gradually changed. After the fateful event with my elder cousin at my uncle's house, my family no longer spent time with our Saudi relatives. And after so many weekend gatherings with my cousins, aunts and uncles, most cousins my age were getting married, many to each other, and my parents felt like our differences became more evident as the children matured into adults. The days of playing hopscotch with my cousins on the sidewalk of their house, playing jacks with small rocks that we hand-picked in the desert, striking *carrom* coins on the wooden floorboard for hours, and painting each other's nails with fancy nail polish, were gone. We tried hard to find common ground. I wondered if for a brief time their efforts were as sincere as mine, but we all knew that intellectual differences were far greater than similarities in our DNA. We spoke differently, we dressed differently, we thought differently, and we even ate differently.

The feasts we experienced at my uncle's house had come to an end. I mourned the disconnect with my relatives, but I didn't miss the uncomfortable ritual: the large and generous spread on the floor with small vegetable bowls placed around the inner parameters of the round floor cloth, with similarly sized and distributed salad bowls. I especially dreaded the confrontation with the huge round tray of rice with a whole *kharoof,* sheep, (including the head) placed on top in the middle.

These gatherings amplified my resentment about gender inequality; the fact that men and boys ate first was a clear message. My mom, who was sold on the lifestyle, was not comfortable with some aspects of these arrangements. She always sent me to spy through a crack in the door of the dining area, "Go see where your father and brother are sitting, so that we can sit in their spot when it's our turn to eat." Everyone used their hands, but my mom was often given a spoon. There were more women and young children than there were men, so we sat a lot more snugly than the men did. My aunt would throw cuts of meat—sometimes brains, other organs or plain chunks of fat—from across the spread towards me, demanding, "EAT! You're too skinny! You need to fatten up!"

In my mid-teens, I witnessed many endings. My relationship with my Saudi relatives was one, but my summers in Italy with my family was another. The first time we visited my mom's place of birth, a village in Southern Italy called Grumento Nova (known simply as Grumento), was the last family vacation because the Gulf War of 1991 changed so many things. Our last family visit was also the first time we had traveled without my older brother and my father. While I didn't have to cover my face or wear the abaya in Italy, my brother usually kept a close eye on his sisters' conduct and behavior. I could not speak to boys, or go too far without a chaperone, and our night curfew was unreasonable for teens in the summertime. Without my brother around, I was determined to stretch my wings and have the time of my life. Without planning to compromise my own personal values, I fully intended to cross his imposing boundaries.

That summer, when we arrived in my mom's hometown of about 2000 people, my sister May and I were the talk of the village. Two exotic Arab girls who were also Italian with family roots in that very village were certainly an oddity that everyone wanted to observe and interact with. We were surrounded by boys who wanted to meet us, and girls who wanted to hang out with us. We formed the best friendships with the boys, easier to do with our older brother not around.

I met a blond, long-haired, hippie guy from Australia, whose Italian mother immigrated to Melbourne with her parents when she was a child, and who spent his summers in this village with his Italian relatives. Max was a surfer and singer, and we felt like kindred spirits with so many things to talk about, in English. I met Giuseppe, who we nicknamed Giosi, a soft spoken, kindhearted young man who, along with his mother, visited his unmarried great aunt Teresina every summer.

During that month in Grumento, we heard stories about old, eccentric Teresina, a woman some called mean and scary. Rumor around the village was that she hoarded her money for decades, and that under her bed, she had money that was no longer in circulation, from before WWII. I watched her take a bucket to the well twice a day, walking up the cobblestone road with a scarf around her head, hunched over and slow, but determined to take advantage of the village well water, since she refused to adjust to modern commodities and more so, pay for such services in her home. One afternoon I asked Giosi "Do you think we can peek into Teresina's house? I am curious about it because everyone seems to think it's so strange." Giosi giggled and suggested a time when he thought his great aunt would be at church.

"Here it is," Giosi said as he invited us in.

Teresina had shut the windows in an attempt to keep the house cool, but all it did was make the house dark, enough of a reason for the village kids to assume it was haunted.

"Can we turn on a light?" I asked.

"She doesn't have electricity in her home," Giosi said.

Just then, Teresina walked into the kitchen. "Welcome," she said warmly, "can I offer you some juice?"

She handed us orange juice in small glasses. The juice was hot, and unpleasant to swallow, but I was committed to making this experience a positive one for me, and especially for Teresina, who despite what everyone said about her, amazed me with her simplicity and genuine generosity of spirit. I respected how much Giosi loved his great aunt regardless of what folks said or thought of her, and I learned for myself to make judgments from my own experience and not sensational rumors.

May and I both had several crushes, but one young man in particular caught my eye with his bad-boy attitude, masterpiece body, and come-hither sense of humor. Franco's family lived next door to my family. His father, who had murdered his wife's accused lover in a fit of rage one night at the bar, now served a life sentence in prison, but was permitted weekend home visits. Franco's mother, who always offered her sweet toothless smile, was a skilled cook. She not only hid the scar of her pain, but also the scar on her chest, inflicted by her husband's attack after he killed her putative lover that fateful night. His clan of siblings, ranging from age twelve to thirty, often congregated at the parents' two-bedroom home.

A modest family of blue-collar workers–like most southern Italian families–they were loud, full of life, and immensely generous. Franco had just graduated from high school with no plans to go to college. He had secured a job as a construction worker, which explained his fit and tanned physique. He rode a motorcycle, which asserted his bad boy image. I knew he had a crush on me too, but I didn't know that he had a girlfriend—and—he didn't know I had a boyfriend in Riyadh.

Just one week before leaving for Italy that summer, I secretly met a young Saudi through a mutual friend. Having no plans to get married any time soon and knowing that there was pending pressure to marry a Saudi man in the near future, I decided I would take action and strategize the path of my destiny as much as possible. I welcomed the innocent and low-pressure relationship with Ahmed, who was born in the U.S. where his Saudi parents lived and where his father received his education and eventually worked. Like me, Ahmed sought a liberal and westernized future partner. We became informally and superficially attached, and with my mom's consent, started a phone relationship to get to know each other better like many modern girls did, secretly.

But I was now in Italy, in a free land, around boys, without my father or brother, for the first time. I was eager to feel like a young woman and wanted to know what it was like to notice boys and be noticed by boys. In the back of my mind, I had a boyfriend, but what did that really mean? I was not in love, in fact, I barely knew him. I was sixteen. I decided I was going to allow myself to live in the moment because I could not be sure that a moment like this would show up again in my life.

Early that month, Franco and I had enjoyed flirting and getting to know each other. Many nights when he came home late, he would climb up the wall into the balcony of my bedroom—in my aunt and uncle's summer home—and bring me pizza.

"We need to be quiet! May is sleeping," I would whisper.

"The stars are as beautiful as you are," he would whisper back while gently massaging my shoulder.

We would sit and talk while we gazed at the sky and nibbled at the pizza. It was beyond what I could have ever imagined possible. This was not Verona, and he was not Romeo, but I felt like Juliet, and we were swooning under the Mediterranean night sky.

One afternoon that summer, Franco and I went on a walk up the hill by the village church and sat behind the church building where we could see the view of the whole village. With the sun behind us, the countryside stretched before us, breathtaking, romantic, and surreal. We sat quietly for several minutes, feeling the wind in our hair, and hearing the chirping of birds. I could feel my heart beating so fast, we were unusually quiet. He moved closer and caressed my hair. I could smell his body through his bright yellow t-shirt. I had never been this close to a boy. Franco sensed my nervous excitement, and without asking, he leaned in and kissed me. My first kiss. In my head I had conflicting thoughts of guilt and shame; to my culture this was blasphemy. In my heart I had feelings of excitement and triumph; in this moment, this was magic.

We never announced to anyone that we were courting one another, but the secret handholding, and the stolen kisses when no one was around kept my heart pounding in thrilling anticipation. For the first time I felt the natural blossoming emotions of desire and curiosity that had been brewing in my head for a couple of years.

During luncheons at my relatives' homes, I could hear Franco's motorcycle race back and forth down the street, his way of letting me know he was around. I enjoyed the attention but felt overwhelmed by his persistence. Still, for several weeks, I embraced the idea that I was experiencing a summer romance and made no effort to turn away opportunities to flirt with other boys and young men in the small and quaint town. Franco was the only boy I kissed that summer, but I savored all the playful, innocent, and enticing encounters I had with some of the other *ragazzi*, the expressive Italian for young guys.

The month of August in Italy is a month of holidays and rest. Many carnivals and festivals take place, and most families take several weeks off from work. In Grumento, we attended traditional Southern Italian celebrations, the festival of the Madonna, Ferragosto, and nighttime carnivals with live music, dancing—where I waltzed with my Zio Bertino for the first time—and of course, food. We strolled around with our friends, ate yummy treats, and bought souvenirs. We laughed and told scary stories in the dark alleys of the village where we also sang and jammed endlessly. I played the drums while Domenico played guitar and Giuseppe played the bass.

One afternoon at the local fair, Franco bought us leather bracelets, his bracelet with my name engraved, mine with his. I was touched and excited by this gesture, until I realized that in his home hung a long chain with dozens of other leather bracelets with girls' names.

"Promise me you won't disappoint me and let your name end up there," he said with a slightly macho tone.

For several days I had been turning away his persistent solicitation for more intimacy, having no interest in losing my virginity before I married. From the start, I knew our summer crush would turn into nothing, but in that moment, I began to lose interest in him. I felt insulted and was reminded of the men and their degrading behavior towards women in my culture. Days after that, I met his girlfriend and knew for sure that our first kiss, and the kisses that followed, along with those sweet nights on the balcony, were now all part of a transformative memory.

His girlfriend Antonietta—who had no idea that her boyfriend and I had flirted for a couple of weeks—had heard about the visiting Arab sisters and was excited to meet us. We found out that she and I share a birthday and a deep love for nature. After that summer Franco and I never spoke again, but Antonietta and I became pen pals. Just a couple of letters into our correspondence, not only did a deep continuing friendship blossom, but I confessed to her what had happened between Franco and me. She was not surprised and told me she had broken up with him because he was dating another girl in another village.

That year marked the end of so many things, including my naiveté. I kissed a boy and was caught in the middle of a teen love-triangle. I spent the last months as a child in the country that gave me so many happy childhood memories, but also a country I could not call home. I transitioned from childhood worries and fears, to the reality of a pending independence that in my culture meant limited personal control and imposed responsibilities.

I experienced the last days of tranquil oblivion as the threat of war from Saddam Hussein rang loud and clear in my country. I never thought I'd know the feeling of life during wartime. I never thought I'd hear alarm sirens wailing in the night and hear missiles land, shaking everything around me. I never thought that the invincible city that I watched grow out of the desert could be vulnerable. If I thought during the past sixteen years of my life that the world was a challenging place, I now knew it. My fears and worries had become more than personal. The prospect of war elevated my sense of instability and heightened my sense of political awareness.

CHANGE IS COMING

After the first night of horror in the capital that had become Saddam Hussein's target, my parents scrambled to find a safer arrangement for us to face the pending dangers of nightly missile attacks. During the day, they confined us to our home, where our windows were covered with tape, and our TV remained on, streaming CNN Live, which, thanks to the presence of U.S. troops, was broadcast through a special satellite, for the first time available to everyone. We spent nights in my father's furniture showroom store basement, safe from the frequent missile attacks where we passed the time reading, playing games, and watching VHS tapes of sitcoms into the late hours of the night.

The resonance of the siren was haunting. I felt knots in my stomach when it would sound. My only reference point to this wailing was from our family's favorite movie, H. G. Wells' *The Time Machine,* when the Morlocks, who lived in the dark undergrounds, would sound a siren—identical to the one I was now hearing at home—to summon the childlike society of the Eloi from the outside, to feed on. Saddam Hussein—like the Morlocks who only surfaced at night—attacked Riyadh after dark, and we spent the early part of 1991 becoming nocturnal for survival.

We were on school break when the threat of war began, which extended our winter hiatus from two weeks to two months. None of us realized that while we celebrated the days off school —and we needed something to celebrate during those times—once we returned, those of us in our senior year would be staying for several hours longer every day of the week, until we covered all the requirements for graduation. It was depressing to start school at 7 am and return home at 7 pm. It was dark, we were exhausted, and had a few hours in the evening remaining to do homework, eat, and sleep, before we had to do it all over again the next day. We went from the jubilation of the end of the short-lived Desert Storm War, to the daily disorientation of what should have been the most exciting and anticipated weeks of our senior year.

The war created a social phenomenon: The heavy presence of the U.S. military had threatened the security of traditional conservative Islamic values as the country suddenly divided between loyal patriots and perceived traitors. Most of our friends, in particular the half-western friends, fled the country to their maternal countries of origin. Some returned after the war ended, although not all. Our family was one of the very few that chose to remain in Riyadh. When I asked my parents why we weren't going to Italy, my mother replied, "This is our country, and we cannot uproot our big family and go to Italy where we have nowhere to stay comfortably."

Her answer struck me as unsatisfactory. Perhaps she was right, but it was a reminder of how much she had chosen to integrate herself and our family in the country that was only half of who we were. She did it for survival, but also because she had deep convictions in her choices. I, on the other hand, had no choice in the matter. I felt like I was brought into this world, shown all the possibilities through inevitable exposure to my other half, but was then firmly told I could not cross the line that was drawn in the sand that separated my two halves. It was perhaps because of this harsh boundary that I never learned to fully accept and appreciate my Arab side.

My best friend Reem and her family also remained in the country during the Gulf War. During the war era, I spent my days with her, in the safety of one of our homes, but at night, we all huddled in our respective designated basement bunkers with our families and various nightly distractions. We were both artistic and creative teens; we played music, we performed in theater, and while my strength was dance, hers was art. This gave Reem and me ways to deal with our worries. Hours went by creating radio shows that we recorded on cassette, for our ears only — today *The Jasmin & Reem Totally Awesome Self-Help Show* would be an epic podcast.

Our talk show addressed current news, social topics, global issues, and of course, we played music. We played the parts of host and guest and took turns making voices and creating characters. One of the segments of our radio show included "calls from listeners," where the caller asked a question, and the answers were delivered in the form of soundbites from some of our favorite songs.

"Yes, I want to know what Bush tell Saddam in the Letter!" I asked playing the part of the caller, speaking broken English with a regional Saudi dialect in a man's voice.

To create the effect of a muffled phone call with static, Reem held my wooden guitar close to the mic and rubbed the back of it with both her hands.

Hothead! Evilution! Nonstop Evilution! By Duran Duran, said it all as the answer to the caller's question played in the form of a song.

It was a very safe and joyful outlet for the two of us. There was no real purpose to what we did, no agenda or goal in mind, other than a way for us to deal with what was going on around us, turning that energy into creative forms. We recorded our show in her room, made home videos with her siblings around the house, did a photoshoot by the swimming pool at my home "That's good! Hold the pose, don't move, I'll run back and put my back against yours!" I said as I pressed the revolutionary self-timer feature of the film camera stacked on a pile of books, which doubled as a tripod. During breaks, we enjoyed delicious snacks: my mom's famous *sambusa*, or the Mexican pizza and chocolate chip cookies that their cook was known for.

I went to school one day, just weeks before the war, and to my surprise Reem was not in class. When I went home and called her to find out why she had missed school, she told me she could not say anything explicitly and instead said, "First letter. Cream. Noodles. Nice." I managed to decode her secret message. She wanted me to turn on CNN—that would explain why she wasn't at school that day. *Saudi Women protest in the streets of Riyadh!*

All over CNN reporters covering the story of 47 Saudi women who drove cars in the heart of the city in a freedom protest, demanding women's right to drive. I understood immediately that Reem and her mom participated in this brave event. I was nervous, I was scared, and I wanted to know everything, but I had no way to talk to my friend. It took a few days before I could finally visit with Reem and get the full story.

"It was mayhem," she said. "It was exciting, and powerful," she continued. "You can't tell anyone about this, we are already facing so many ramifications."

I listened to her with so much pride. "I wish I was there with you all," I confessed, then added, "It would have been worth the horrible aftermath."

That historic deed opened the door to the subsequent documented efforts for women's rights in the Kingdom, and almost thirty years later, Saudi women were finally granted the right to drive. It came at a high price, as the families of these brave women suffered immense consequences— then and now. They experienced house arrest and lost their right to travel outside of the country for years. Their phones were tapped, and they were surveilled, forced to sign gag orders and pledges that any defiant attempt against the government would never take place in the future. Some of the women who took part in this bold movement continue, to this day, to live with constant backlash and threat.

Through my youthful and inexperienced lens, I knew something was happening to the world around me. I could not articulate the confusion that I sensed as I watched our local news glorify President George H. Bush, General Norman Schwarzkopf Jr., and Secretary of Defense, Dick Cheney. Those names were heard and spoken in every household in the region.

In the malls, images of U.S. soldiers in military uniform excited me, as I liked being surrounded by the potent American culture, even as the soldiers remained respectful and reserved in the midst of this foreign land. But nothing gave me a bigger thrill than seeing the American women in military uniforms walking stoically and heroically. I was in awe and wanted to approach every single one of those women, but I didn't, I couldn't.

I don't think I realized how dramatic that whole shift in our social structure was while it was happening right in front of me. The visual presence of the American troops—which to some felt like an invasion—alongside the established traditional cultural norms, felt like a threatening clash. But at school, we decided to take advantage of these current events and created a play that reenacted, in a witty and comedic fashion, a famous Saudi TV show about male Bedouin poets in the desert, with a twist. The episode we portrayed included a fictional special guest, a U.S. soldier stationed in Riyadh: I was cast in the part of Corporal Jim-Bob Lou Jr, a name I pilfered from an episode of *Three's Company*.

During these months of uncertainty, I became aware of perks in the world beyond the Atlantic Ocean. Using satellite TV, many of us in Saudi Arabia tuned in to the programs provided to the U.S. military bases. I watched *Saturday Night Live, The Simpsons*, and my personal favorite, *The Tonight Show* with Jay Leno as Carson's sub just a year before he took the seat as permanent host. Up until that point, my exposure to Western culture had a strong European strain. Although already familiar with American popular culture through music and movies, I became a consumer in a current and immediate way. American life enthralled me, and I became smitten with the American experience, enamored with the tangible presence of the American clout in my daily life.

It was perhaps during this crucial and influential time, unbeknownst to me, that my love-affair with America began.

THE SECRET

Puberty changes everything overnight. Young adolescents suffer the consequences of abiding strict Islamic laws and rules as do adults. Now an adolescent making adult decisions, I began to wonder how the algorithmic formula that worked in society for many, would work for me: childhood, abaya, high school, engagement, college and/or marriage. I was sixteen when I met my first boyfriend, a surprisingly uneventful affair that was overshadowed by my encounter with the boy with whom I would share my first kiss in Italy.

Ahmed was seventeen, had just graduated high school, and had been living in Saudi Arabia less than three years. He was born and raised in New York, where his Saudi father—an exceptionally benevolent man in a culture where most men tend to be reserved—went to college and later worked for the Saudi Consulate in the United Nations. His Saudi mother was a housewife with limited education but with sharp social and cultural intelligence. She was also a phenomenal cook. Ahmed was highly westernized and struggling to acclimatize to his new Saudi life. His family originated from the Western Region of Hijaz, which made them automatically more progressive and liberal than the central region Saudis of Najd, where I grew up, and where he now lived.

Ahmed and I were both seeking a romantic relationship of our choosing, one that would save us from the obligatory arranged marriage. He wanted an open-minded young woman with whom he could be himself. And since my only option was to marry a Saudi man, I wanted to find one who was either bicultural like myself or educated in the West.

Having never been in a relationship before, neither one of us knew what it was to be in love, so we came to the arrangement with naive expectations. We acted deeply in love even before we really had a chance to know one another. We forced expressions of passion, reacted in jealousy when it was totally unnecessary, and wrote long and poetic love letters to one another. We were most honest with each other when we dwelled on the injustice of our inability to have a normal romance. Our common ground was our Western background and generational interests, which meant we enjoyed the same music, movies, and pop-culture fads. We became great friends, with a forced and artificial love story.

Within the first few weeks, we decided that this relationship was destined for marriage. It would be a traditional marriage that concealed our non-traditional circumstances, an unspoken determination masterfully orchestrated by each of us to survive the expectation of our culture. He was ready to experience life as a man with all the perks that come with that, including having a romantic, sexual, and life partner—I wanted my freedom.

By now I had accepted the reality that thinking of marriage was the only aspiration for a girl my age in our society. Unlike my friends who were openly discussing their plans and waiting for a suitor, I was hypocritically making plans to pave the most convenient path for my future. The first year of our relationship was a struggle. We never saw each other, spoke only occasionally on the phone, and our teenage interests and friends distracted us, including my temporary liberty while in Italy on vacation. I was still in high school; he was in college; outside of those secret phone calls, we had no other way to relate. Planning to talk on the phone was a complex production. After my mom found out that I had met this young man, she encouraged me to be discreet in how I interacted with him, and to be clear about the outcomes of this relationship. Life began for most young women after marriage; I was not itching to get married, but I was ready to become an adult.

We met in the early part of the summer, just one week before that fateful trip to Italy, where I tasted the freedom of adulthood without my father and brother around. I attended live concerts and soccer games for the first time, stayed up late walking up and down the central avenue of the village and met distant relatives and cousins of whom I had only heard of from the elders in my family. I watched the old ladies of the south make homemade pasta, biscotti, and liquor. I learned to gather water from the local well across from my aunt's house, and thanks to peer influences, I immediately adopted the charming dialect of the South. When I went down that list in my mind, I had no regrets and no guilt; even months later when I received love letters from a twenty-three-year-old I met that summer, I welcomed this attention, noting that this reminder of summer felt more authentic than what I was trying to engineer with Ahmed.

I was back to my ordinary odd life, and to my secret boyfriend, after having lived so simply and so fully just weeks before. Preceding our departure from Italy, I downloaded into my bones all the sensations I felt that summer. I wanted to have them for safekeeping when I needed a memento of how beautifully free life can be. The arid desert of home threatened to dry those memories. The first few weeks after returning, I needed the letters to and from Italy, the cassette recordings with the summer's hit list on a loop in my boombox, and the gallery of photographs in my albums to rehydrate myself.

That fall, I resumed a committed relationship with Ahmed, mostly in my head. I was not as taken as the day I met him just weeks before, but since I knew this was going to be a one in a million chance to marry someone who would allow me some autonomy, I played along. It took effort and compartmentalization.

Getting to know Ahmed gave me the opportunity to relate to men. I didn't have much practice with my introverted father and my independent brother. My relationship with Yasser was always civil. We respected one another, but I resented his position in the family and society. He was given many privileges and—while he never exercised it—had authority over his own mother, by law. Yasser was assertive, cocky, and extremely charismatic. Many of my friends had a crush on him, which of course made me want to gag. The truth was, I admired him and longed for his approval, but I also despised his entitlement and sought ways to rebel against him.

By now, only my mom and May knew about my four-month relationship with Ahmed. One evening when I was on the phone with him, Yasser picked up the handset in another room and heard the voice of a male. He said nothing, hung up and left the house. I was terrified about what his silence meant. Thankfully, this privileged brother of mine had a pager, so I paged him because I needed to calm the state of hyperventilation, I was in.

When he called me back, his voice was aloof and calm, "Yes?" he asked.

"I know you heard me on the phone with a boy, when you come home, can we talk about it, please?" I begged nervously.

To my surprise he remained levelheaded and said, "Okay."

When Yasser was home late that night, I approached his room, my heart pounding, and my nerves on edge, but I was determined to speak my truth to him. At his door, I knocked.

"Come in," he called out.

I went inside. Yasser was sitting in his usual spot on the bed close to his phone, facing the TV. The familiar mess of books and cassettes around his room calmed my anxious gaze.

I took a breath. "I want to talk to you about that phone call you overheard. I know you are upset. I need you to believe that Mamma is aware and has been monitoring my actions. Ahmed and I aren't doing anything wrong. We plan to marry."

Yasser watched me while I talked, silent. When I finished, he said, "I am not angry and I don't mind, as long as you have a goal in mind, and not just messing around with a boyfriend. I want to meet him and assess his intentions. I know you will not marry any old traditional Saudi man, and I am not opposed to this choice you made. I just want to make sure it is all in accordance with our family's values."

Despite his cultural rant, our dialogue, which was always in Italian, reflected the true nature of our family's morals and our parents' modern attitudes. Initially in shock at having been discovered, I was now beyond relieved; his response epitomized the depth of trust Yasser and I shared and which, over the years, through the ups and downs, has proven to be a fundamental strength for our family.

"So, you're okay with Ahmed and I continuing to talk on the phone?" I asked.

Yasser nodded. "Keep it to once a week," he said. "And limit the calls to a half hour each."

I wanted to protest, to tell him it was not his concern how often or how long Ahmed and I spoke on the phone, but I knew better than to cross him. I could see that he relished his authority over me, but since I got what I wanted from him, and planned on doing things my way anyway, I played along.

IDENTITY

After the war and high school, I began college in the linguistics department of King Saud University for girls in Riyadh. The college campus was huge and overwhelming. Most of the buildings were old and unkept, a drastic difference from my beautifully prestigious private school for the past decade. At the university there were young women from all backgrounds and walks of life. The majority were traditional, conservative Saudi women from public schools. I was in the minority, not only as a private school graduate but also as a mixed breed. I attracted a lot of attention, more than I was comfortable with. Although I had sought attention in my youth for my dance and performances, I became self-conscious because I knew my classmates' interest in me stemmed from the wrong reasons. Repeatedly, other students asked if I was Saudi. My brief answer, "yes," never seemed enough for them. Because I was too fair complexioned to be Saudi, they wanted to know if I was Lebanese or Syrian. My answers never satisfied them, and they pried further and further:

"Is your father Saudi?"

"Yes," I sighed.

"Where is your father's family from?"

"Hail," was my answer, which is as traditionally Saudi as it can get.

"Where is your mother from?"

Without making eye contact, "Italy," I would say.

"Well WHY didn't you say so? That's why you look like that!"

"Look like what?" I would ask.

"Your body is European, your features are not boldly Arab, your skin is too pale…it's because you are not a pure Saudi!"

One day, the intrigue of my identity went so far that I was asked a question which opened a whole new door to my world of identification:

"Are you *Gabeeli* or *Khadheeri?*"

My head reeled internally, *ummm, come again?* "I'm not sure I understand your question?"

"Oh well, if you don't know the answer, then you must be *Khadheeri,*" was the comeback.

I guess I must be *whatever that is.*

I went home that day and asked my father, "are we *Gabeeli* or *Khadheeri?*"

"Why do you ask?" he said indignantly.

"A girl at the University asked me," I said.

"Don't hang out with people who ask such stupid questions. You have no business being around such individuals."

"OK, but why? What do those words mean?" I insisted.

"It's nonsense, don't engage in these conversations!" He said, as he walked away.

I guess we must be Khadeeri, like that girl said, is that a bad thing? I thought.

I went to Yasser and asked him the same question and, finally, an answer, "A person who is *Gabeeli* has tribal origins, meaning, his ancestors can be traced to a known tribe in Saudi Arabia; on the other hand, a *Khadheeri* person, is an Arab without known tribal origins, often because the family came from other parts of the Arabian Peninsula or other Arab countries in the region without strong tribal identities."

"So, what are we?" I asked, not really invested in the outcome of the answer. Yasser hesitated and said, "I'm really not sure, because all Arabs are part of a tribe, but most likely we are *Khadheeri.*"

Finally, it was clear. We were not pure in any sense.

Now I knew more of who I was. I also knew that my brother trusted my vision for my future and having his approval of my relationship with Ahmed meant the battle was half won. If Yasser and my mother saw him as a fit future husband, my father would be an easier wheel to grease. While my father would not have been distracted by the purity of a mate for his daughters, his real concern was the family name, because in society that mattered. Ahmed's mother, on the other hand, was quite traditional and not fond of the idea of having a half-Western wife for her son. She believed if we had kids, one day I would take off with them, and go to Europe, leaving her son behind as had happened to a relative of theirs who was—coincidentally—married to a Western woman. She hoped for a more culturally compatible daughter-in-law, and struggled with the differences between us, including the fact that I didn't eat meat.

Ahmed shared with me a conversation that his mom had on the phone with her sister after meeting me for the first time. She exclusively described my aesthetic strengths and weaknesses, as if she had just visited an equestrian stable to select the prize horse she wanted to take home: "Yes, she has fair skin, yes, she has a European look. Her hair is long, straight, and dark, but she is too thin and doesn't look pure Arab."

After I met Ahmed's extended family, I realized why those details mattered so much to them. The family, which was of noble origins descending from the Islamic Prophet's heritage, looked like the United Colors of Benetton. Both grandmothers were of Asian origins, which was visible in Ahmed's features. He had cousins who were black, brown, and white, the offspring of the multiple pilgrim wives of their great-grandfathers. The family valued Arab Caucasian features the most. When I met Ahmed's 100-year-old, debilitated Malaysian great-grandmother for the first time, she kissed me and said six words in broken Arabic, the only six words she ever said to me, "God-bless, long nose! Good babies!"

Where I grew up, I was always considered light-skinned, because when you live indoors, and never spend time in the sun, you are more likely to look like a vampire, especially if you are genetically half-European. One of my Saudi friends, who had striking bronze skin and sharp dark features, used to call me cotton-bud. In the West, where I am unveiled, I miss no opportunity to be in the sun, soaking up vitamin D and breathing the fresh air. Because of this, I am labeled an exotic-olive-skinned peculiarity from the Middle East.

It took twenty years for me to learn that the racial definitions in the United States are based in deep ignorance and awkward history, certainly not global anthropological research. I grew up having a strong and solid sense of my racial identity. My ethnicity was problematic and confusing to me, but my race was never in question. Both my parents are Caucasian. My father was a light-skinned Arab, and my mother was a sun-kissed Mediterranean brunet. My parents did not look like a biracial couple, and, in fact, they didn't look like a bi-ethnic couple either. I was a *white* child, who did not know the meaning or existence of race, let alone white privilege. It was only much later in my adolescence that I became aware of race as an aspect of identity because I heard people talk about it and saw it portrayed in movies, especially American movies.

Outside of the United States, white signifies Caucasian, as distinguished from African and Asian. In America I have come to learn, after many years of confusion and research, that "Caucasian" means "Northern European white." While a very light-skinned black person in American is still considered black, a darker-skinned Caucasian person, like me, is NOT considered white. This I have learned from the confused people of this obscure nation. People have referred to me as bi-racial, or Person of Color, projecting their own assumptions while simultaneously displaying their sad and deep-rooted ignorance of this troubling issue. When all skin tones have flexibility under minority labels, and white is based on only one tone, it is the foundation of ignorance, racism, and racial insensitivity. I remain convinced this is an American phenomenon rooted in the horrific history of slavery.

Ultimately, I never care how people view me and I rarely correct them, unless appropriate, but even when I do, it still doesn't seem to make sense to them, or resonate for very long, because when my tan lasts from June to May, it must mean that I have some eccentric racial metamorphic gene.

As a child playing on the beaches, it didn't matter how dark I got because tanning was an expression of freedom. It was only as I grew older, and traveled to America, that the seasonal changes in the color of my skin became racialized.

SPIRITUAL AWAKENING

It took two years before Ahmed and I got engaged.

"I feel like this nightmare will never end!" I would often say in the early months of our private relationship during our infrequent phone calls.

His reassuring words offered some degree of comfort, "We are meant to be together, no matter how long it takes. We are working hard to achieve that. I will continue to talk to my parents about my readiness for marriage."

During those two years I finished high school and started college, as he proceeded with his college studies and part time work. In the two years of our unofficial courtship, our families supervised us while remaining uninvolved. The formality of our engagement was subdued compared to traditional customs. Because we both knew each other and essentially chose one another, our parents did not have much work to do, other than oblige and go through the motions. The engagement was merely a way to let society know that we were betrothed.

As an engaged couple our meetings always included a family chaperone, usually my mother and her book. Before our official wedding, we had an Islamic ceremony called *Milkah*, a legal contract-signing event performed by an Imam. The contract transfers the ownership of the young woman from her father to her husband.

"Here you go," Yasser said, handing me a large stack of cash, "Your dowry. Papa looked so sad when Ahmed and his father handed it to him and he asked me to bring it to you immediately," he continued. "I think it was hard on him, he seemed emotional about the symbolism of the exchange."

I was moved and sad at the thought of my father's realization. "This feels so strange, I don't know how to feel about it either," I confessed.

The contract-signing event took place at our home. Only the men participated, while I remained upstairs in my bedroom waiting for updates on how it was going.

I understood my father's pain. The event was a wake-up call since I was his first daughter to marry. The word *milkah* originates from *moolk*, which means ownership or property. The root word *malik/malek* which means king, refers to the fact that a king owns the land and its many prosperities. The purpose of the *milkah* ceremony is to ultimately facilitate the opportunity for the couple to spend time alone legally and unsupervised to prepare a home and get to know each other.

Until the official wedding, the expectation was that both bride and groom would remain virgins. On the wedding night—also known as "*dukhlah*," which literally means *entering*— the couple consummate their marriage and engage in their first sexual encounter. I knew many couples who did not wait for the wedding night once they performed the *Milkah*, which was not illegal or an Islamic sin, but was culturally immoral and remained a concealed activity. Ahmed was a rule follower, and I was not particularly eager at that point to explore all sexual aspects of a relationship. In retrospect, I understand my reticence as a sign that I was not madly in love, nor even in lust or passionately awakened. That feeling came much later, with another man.

During the months of our *milkah*, we hunted for an apartment, furniture shopped, and planned our small wedding and honeymoon. For me the sole purpose of our union was to travel and live our adult lives, which after all, most unmarried couples our age around the world could do without being legally bound. Those days of planning were happy times. I was finally unburdened from my father and brother's lawful control, which was never harsh but a pending pressure in the back of my mind limiting my choices in life. Although my husband was now my legal guardian, he was the openminded partner I wanted. I gained a small sense of independence as a woman, where my say was *almost* as important as his.

A few months after the *milkah*, we celebrated an intimate wedding with our parents, siblings, and housekeepers. That same night, we flew to Italy for our month-long honeymoon. Ahmed met my Italian family, and I think he felt the way I often did around his relatives—a desire to belong, with an obvious sense of loss and misplacement. These were not his people, this was not his country, he did not speak the language or understand the customs. Although he didn't resent my place in this culture, he struggled to find common ground.

At dinner one night in a romantic candle-lit restaurant in Venice, the maître d' was astonished at the fact that we were married because of how young we looked.

Knowing that my husband did not speak Italian, he asked me, bursting into sarcastic laughter, "Explain to me why a beautiful Italian girl like you is married to such an ugly Filipino guy?"

I was shocked and offended, and when Ahmed asked me what was said, I translated, "He asks what an Italian girl like me has in common with a Filipino guy?" leaving out the words "beautiful" and "ugly," making it sound more like a question of linguistic incompatibility.

"Tell him I am not Filipino, but I am a lucky man to be with you!" Ahmed said with a huge grin.

I forced a smile and looked at the rude maître d', saying "I think my husband is very handsome!"

I knew it had been a racist remark. Ahmed looked racially mixed; he also did not fit the standard of good looks for either European or Middle Eastern men: he was not tall, his features did not show strong masculine qualities as he lacked facial hair, and his youthful ambiguity made him more of a boy than a man. Ahmed was exotically handsome, and it was painful to witness the blatant discrimination towards his Asian features. I began to understand why he resented his Malaysian grandmother and felt the impulse to frequently mention that he was a descendent of the prophet Mohammed, asserting his genetic origins.

I enjoyed the feeling of independence but also panicked when I realized that I was now married with pending expectations to start a family. I cared about Ahmed, but I was not in love with him. Starting a family with someone who had different beliefs concerned me. How could I have children when I was preoccupied with such nonsense as "adjusting the racial genes," thus fulfilling his mother's bizarre wish for me to "improve" the bloodline? What if I had a child and that child looked Asian? Will I be the only one to love my baby? What if we started a family, and one day, I met my soul mate? These thoughts became intrusive and inescapable. All I knew was that I would hold off on having a child as long as possible, or as long as we lived in Saudi Arabia.

I had heard stories of custody battles and seen the movie *Not Without My Daughter*, based on the true story of Betty Mahmoody, an American woman married to an Iranian man. After being manipulated into visiting her husband's family in Iran, Betty and her daughter became captives, held against their will, prompting her to fight a long custody battle, including separation from her daughter. She subsequently fled back to the U.S. with her daughter and with an entire country on her side, ready and willing to fight for her constitutional rights. As a Saudi woman married to a Saudi man, I had no rights to my children if I decided to change the course of my life. That was Islamic law. I laid my fears to rest, as Ahmed and I agreed to postpone having children for several years, so that he could explore graduate school and decide where we would ultimately live. We both acknowledged the fact that we were too young and wanted to travel and have fun before settling down with kids.

I became a presumed Muslim wife without being religious. I was, in fact, never drawn to the Islamic teachings as a way of life—or any other organized religious teachings for that matter. To voice such thoughts in Saudi Arabia could lead to the ultimate punishment, death. Nevertheless, I chose to live like a modern, casually devout Muslim. My mother, who was deeply immersed in metaphysical studies and Eastern based philosophies, had an open-door policy since I was a child that continued to influence my beliefs as an adult. The subjects of God and religion were tricky however, because she recognized that an Islamic upbringing would avoid confusion and societal backlash. For my part, it was impossible to deny the transformational need to seek.

When Ahmed would ask me to join him in prayer I would oblige, but my mind would wander to the times that I hopped on my mom's bed after her afternoon nap and without any warning posed to her the many existential questions I had. She was a wonderful listener, and a comforting sounding board. On the other hand, I would remember how my father never expressed any thought or opinion on matters beyond the mundane facts of daily life. He was traumatized by the stunning disappointments and rejection he encountered from a society he naively believed—as a young man—was interested in his intellectual awakening after his western education. Like many of his colleagues who studied abroad, he expected to blend the educational ideologies of the West with the traditional values of his culture; but the country and its people were not ready. My siblings and I took after our deep-thinking, vocal mother and were troubled by the big questions, or at least curious about other ways of thinking as we also came to terms with the set expectations laid out before us by society. My fifteen minutes of prayer were spent daydreaming, recollecting how my own family practiced—or didn't practice—religion.

I once asked my mom, "What *really* is the purpose of life?"

She said, "To be happy, and productive, and experience life and all that it has manifested, in order to grow spiritually and evolve."

"Yeah," I said with an exasperated sigh, while I laid upside down on the armchair, with my feet over its back and my head dangling to the ground. "But THIS is not a life," I added, referring to the shallow, empty, and oppressed one that I was living.

I have come to understand that oppression creates the same damage in all who experience any form of it. It robs you of your truth. I can empathize with what some folks in the LGBTQIA+ community feel. They are raised forcefully to accept that the default societal path of a heterosexual life and marriage is the only right way, even when it is an unauthentic existence. I was never given the opportunity to evaluate my spiritual truth: I was *told* what I was. By law, as a Saudi citizen, the default religion I am to practice is

Islam, even though I was also Italian and entitled to explore Catholicism. My Saudi identity took precedence and there was no way to negotiate with this level of oppression. In all cases, the oppressed face severe repercussions.

Married life plunged me into the cultural and religious reality that I observed from the safety of my unorthodox upbringing. For generations, my husband's family was deeply involved in the proceedings of the Islamic pilgrimage, or *Hajj*. They owned a business that helped assist and aid pilgrims from Southeast Asia during the annual event that welcomes over two million pilgrims from around the world. The Islamic pilgrimage is carried out over the course of about a week, but the preparations begin a month before that. I was surprised to learn that within the first year of our marriage, it was my duty, in the eyes of my in-laws, to fulfill my Islamic pilgrimage. I knew this was one of the pillars for every able-bodied Muslim in their lifetime to perform during the designated month of the lunar Hijra calendar; but I did not anticipate how soon I would prepare for it. My family never talked about this grand undertaking.

It was not the first time I had laid eyes on the Holy Kaaba. During our engagement, my then future in-laws took me to perform my first *Umrah*—the non-mandatory mini-pilgrimage that can be performed more than once and at any time of the Hijra calendar year. My first impression of the Kaaba was of sheer awe. This was a magnificent building. The black box that I always saw on TV seemed more than just a black box. What was stunning to me was the aura around the Kaaba, and its size, almost 630 square feet and forty feet in height. The closer I got to it, the better I could see the original stone building preserved, under the recognizable black cloth, ornamented with phrases from the Koran embroidered with gold thread. Surrounded by heavy silver and inlaid in one of the corners was the Black Stone of Mecca; it is said that this stone dates back to Adam and Eve.

As the pilgrim unit circumambulated the Kaaba, each one of those hundreds of thousands of individuals strived to touch the Black Stone. Few were successful, and when they were, the evident agony in their tears and wails told stories of despair and helplessness. The sight of people from all walks of life unified in the sacred space moved me to tears. The Kaaba sits in the center of the Holy Mosque, known as *Al-Haram,* which today has been completely reconstructed to accommodate about 300,000 worshippers at a time. The contractors for this and other major construction expansions in the Kingdom is the Bin Laden Family Group, the family of origin of Osama Bin Laden, and who have publicly condemned Osama's path.

I had seen the Vatican before, and even as a young child, it took my breath away. I visited many Catholic Churches in Italy, from the Duomo in Milan to the Basilica of St. Francis of Assisi, to St. Mark's Basilica in Venice and the Cathedral of Santa Maria Del Fiore in Florence. These consequential edifices tell stories of civilizations long gone, and centuries of spiritual, as well as political, evolution. Perhaps because of the collective energy of hope, prayer, and redemption that mankind has conjured, these holy sites invoke awe even to those of us who are not seeking spiritual refuge. The historic significance of these timeless representations has always reminded me of our humanity and deep desire for purpose.

The *Umrah* experience was a meaningful and peaceful one. As it is intended to be, the *Hajj* journey was rich in challenges, setbacks, and even disturbing events. Although it is mandatory only for the able-bodied, many frail people undertake the pilgrimage. In the crowds of millions, many die from heat, dehydration, and occasional stampedes. There are also horrific violations by individuals who take advantage of the circumstances by either pickpocketing, or molesting women, young girls, and boys.

Women performed the *Hajj* rituals in silence. Men chanted prayers. We walked from site to site following the sacred route. The heat was tempered by the fact that everyone was dressed in white. I held on to the characteristic draping that wrapped Ahmed, for fear of losing him. The smell of unbathed bodies—sweat, urine, flatulence, rotting food, vomit—was unbearable. And yet, genuine toothless smiles by elders greeted me, the disabled offered prayers, and energetic toddlers, who wanted to help their families, sold snacks and toys. It was a micro globe. A functioning ecosystem amid chaos and hustle.

"How long do you think this ritual will take?" I asked Ahmed, whispering in his ear for fear of being heard.

"I am not sure, there are so many people, but we can fight our way to the front," he answered, grabbing my hand, and pushing forward.

Concerned, I asked "It's so hard to see all those fainted bodies, are they going to be okay?" I wondered if I too was going to be okay. Each day was getting harder and harder to face.

"Don't worry, they will be taken care of, just focus on what we have to do," he said. In his tone I detected the anticipation of more hardship.

At one particular rite we were performing, I felt an unusual closeness behind me, someone pressing against my back, aiming for contact with my backside. Before I could react, I felt a hand reaching between my legs, and in horrified rage I turned around. Without waiting to look the pervert in the eye, I punched him in the face as hard as I could. When my husband realized what had happened, he became unhinged, spewing profanities in rage, while his father held him back and reminded him that *Hajj* was about facing sacrificial challenges, and that God is watching.

I was traumatized by the event, and by the fact that my sweet father-in-law viewed this undeserved violation as a test from "God," and a blessing—an occasion for my husband and me to practice our faith, as real Muslim martyrs.

The *Hajj* had positive life-changing moments, too. The experience ignited my spiritual seeking, even beyond Islam, and certainly beyond religion. On the historic day of Arafah, where pilgrims walk several miles at dawn from Mina to Mount Arafah in total silence and meditative contemplation, I found myself, probably for the first time in my life, awakened to the higher divinity, what felt like the universal greatness. I caught a glimpse into the collective oneness. The sun was rising with a deep red glow against the sand and dunes of this preserved uninhabited land. To witness hundreds of thousands, if not millions, of men, women, and children, of all races and ethnicities, walking in the Arabian desert in harmony and serenity, many in tears but all in calm, committed reverence was a truly heartrending image, one that I often borrow during my own meditations.

WORLD TRAVELER

My husband and I loved traveling, and our trips to the West offered a glimpse into the tangible adult life that I pined for. During most of the year, we chose to live quite modestly in order to save our money for summer and winter travels. In the early years of our marriage, we visited a few countries in the Arabian Peninsula, as well as many cities along the Mediterranean, both in Southern Europe and Northern Africa. Although I had traveled extensively in Italy, most of what I knew lay in the north. With Ahmed I went back to Naples, the pulse of southern Italian culture, where I only passed through as a young teen with my family. In Naples, there's the good, the bad, and the ugly. The food is delicious, the people are loud, the city streets are littered, and its reputation of high-risk crime is viewed by the locals as fiction.

The first time I visited Naples, I was with my family, and I wanted to find the home of my favorite Italian singer, Edoardo Bennato, the pride of *Bagnoli*, a suburb of Naples. Known as the Dylan of Italy, Bennato, is a storyteller with masterful songwriting skills. This one-man-band played his guitar, tambourine, and harmonica all at once, as he sang songs of philosophical depth and social injustices, sometimes comically with a hint of prophetic wisdom. After asking around this small village—which we detoured through to satisfy my fangirl demands that my family tolerated and humored—we managed to find the building where Bennato's mother lived. Her name clearly displayed on the intercom of the main gate. I rang and rang—not quite sure what the outcome of that unsolicited visit would be—but Mrs. Bennato was not home. I settled for a pose and photo in front of the building where I imagined Edoardo visited often to see his Mamma.

When Ahmed and I arrived at the Naples port to board for a weeklong Mediterranean cruise, the few hours in Naples were terrifying. I felt the responsibility of being the communicator for the two of us, thus extra alert for any sign of potential danger. Ahmed was nervous too, aware that we had far too many suitcases, that he looked like a foreigner, and that we both looked like we were sixteen. We got off the train at the station by the port, confused young tourists—*perfect targets*, I thought. Before too long, a bald gentleman, riding a motorized cart, approached us and offered us a ride for a nominal fee to the ship docking area. With all the luggage we had in tow, this was a good idea. We hopped on, Ahmed in the back to keep his eyes and hands on our luggage and I in the front next to the driver. The driver was a native of Naples, his dialect melodically delicious. He was oozing Southern Italian charm, with mischief that kept me on guard.

"Where are you guys from?" he asked.

I hate this question. "I'm Arab-Italian, he's Arab-American," I said, hesitantly.

"Woh! ARAB? What Arab country?" He asked curiously.

Yuck, THAT question, I thought. "Saudi Arabia," I mumbled.

"So, are you the daughter of a Sheik?" His eyes lit up.

Great! He thinks I'm loaded. "NO! NO! NO! I'm … the daughter of … nobody," I replied, without giving my answer any thought, until after the words came out of my mouth. *YAY! Now he thinks I'm a bastard child of a poor Italian woman!*

But the driver was a smart man and picked up on my embarrassment as well as my obvious fear. He laughed and said, "What about him, is he also the son of nobody?" I thought, for sure, he had figured out that we were total idiots, and he was going to rob us during the short drive.

When we finally arrived at the dock, he helped us down, held my hand and said, after he kissed it, "Don't believe everything they say about us Napoletani. There are bad apples in every bunch. You have nothing to worry about, you are safe, and if you give this city a chance, you will fall in love with it and its people. Have a wonderful trip!"

He did not let us pay him.

I learned from this man not to let societal imposition of stereotypes cloud my judgment. He was a true angel; someone who, by his good deed, changed the course of someone else's life.

Of the few parts of Italy I hadn't visited before, Sicily was one. With Ahmed, I finally explored Palermo, a charming port city, that shockingly depicted a visual clashing of my two cultures. With historic Arab invasions, Palermo's people, buildings, and even written signs, mirrored the strong Muslim and Arab influences. For this reason, I think Ahmed really enjoyed Palermo and Barcelona, where there too, we saw the undeniable imprint of the Muslim Moors. In Barcelona, however, I was mesmerized by the prominence of Gaudí's art and architecture visible all over the city, from The Casa Batlló, an impossible-to-describe fantastical dream-like design of homes and balconies resembling colorful masks, to the enchanting Park Güell, and his unfinished, gothic Sagrada Família Temple. Touring these beautiful places was not only a destination-traveling adventure, but a time-traveling adventure as well. To be in any location, without imagining what it looked like hundreds or thousands of years ago and picture individuals of that world going about their daily lives, walking on the very same spot I now stood, is a privilege that documents the human story to which I owe my sense of self. This practice of mental travel began when I went to Pompeii for the first time with my family, and continued just as powerfully the second time, when I took Ahmed to see it. The burning questions of our existence that I posed to my mother and discussed with my siblings, were aired out when I visited these places.

Revisiting Pompeii, now as an adult, I was alerted to the fact that this is a site where change is inevitable, whether it is a spiritual awakening, an existential exploration, a fascination with nature's preservation, or a reconciliation with the magnificence of ancient civilizations.

When walking down the avenues of this once buried village, I experienced humanity at a molecular level. I stared at the famous petrified dog, wondering what kind of pet it was, who its family was, or if maybe it was just a stray? The sad sight of the family lying asleep—which included a baby and toddler—engulfed in lava and memorialized as statues forever, forewarned me of how fragile we are, and yet how eternal our imprint on history is. So many stories that we'll never know, what did their voices sound like? What made them laugh and cry? What were their hidden talents and passions in life? One day these questions will be asked of our civilization, but as we become a technologically advanced society, always eager to objectify our value with impulsive changes and replacements—with such a disposable legacy—what will remain of us to ignite similar questions by future humans?

As a teen, when I visited Pompeii the first time, I was not allowed to enter a particular part of the ruins because it included "adult content." I was curious and frustrated and wanted to know what was there, and, why I was not allowed to see what was so appealing that adults would stand in long lines to see it. When I returned with Ahmed, now an adult in my own right, I beelined to that spot as soon as we arrived. After standing in that long line, we entered the forbidden buildings where I was gravely disappointed to encounter nothing more than Roman erotica: many phalluses depicted in wall paintings, bronze amulets and ceramic carvings, and the pornographically decorated walls of brothels and basilicas. In my curious, philosophical, idealist mind, I had been hoping to uncover the secrets of the universe, and the meaning of life.

It was hard to believe that during my life before marriage, I had never visited any other Arab country besides the one I lived in. The Arab world is an extremely diverse and historically rich gem, nestled perfectly in the middle of the ancient world. My father was not comfortable having our family around other Arabs, because of the amount of work it took to conform. While we could present as the Arab-Italian-modern-liberal family that we were at home, my father's preoccupation with what people thought required us to present the public image of reserved-respectful-law-abiding-Saudis. In the end, my father preferred not to deal with that, something I knew because when we traveled to Europe, he instructed us to speak Italian, act Italian and not acknowledge Arabs in public, especially in Switzerland, where in the 1980s, rich Saudis flocked.

So, there I was, an educated Arab adult whose only understanding of the Arab experience was the highly conservative and reserved Saudi one. Ahmed and I changed that. We both had a curiosity about other Arab countries. During our Mediterranean cruise, we visited Sidi Bou Said, a town in northern Tunisia and the first Arab country outside of Saudi Arabia that I had visited. This quaint and charismatic port town seemed like a reflection from across the Mediterranean Sea, where the extensive use of white and blue in its architecture resembles the Greek islands of Santorini and Sikinos. The hybrid Arabic they spoke was hard to understand, and the modesty of their lifestyle was like a scene in a movie. In Sidi Bou Said, everyday life moved slowly, while the tourists moved fast. Store merchants lured shoppers with competitive prices and local goods. The smell of spices and dried fruit was exquisite, and the scraggly smiles of many of the old wrinkled-copper-skinned men who sat drinking tea and smoking the hookah, was a beautiful introduction to a different Arab world from the one I knew.

Next on our Arab country list was Bahrain. This was the 1990's, and the rapper, Coolio, had taken over the world with his hit "Gangsta's Paradise." When we found out that Coolio was performing a show in Bahrain, we set out for a visit. We made the short drive across King Fahad Causeway, the long bridge that ties the Eastern Province of the Kingdom with Bahrain, a tiny island country in the middle of the Persian Gulf. Many Saudis spend weekends in Bahrain, where the families enjoy picnics on the beach and deprived young men indulge in alcohol and women gazing. Bahrain can be explored in hours by car. I was amazed at the population, which looked primarily South Asian, mainly Indian. It did not appear to be the rich country I thought it was. The gap between poverty—which was visible on the streets and local areas—and wealth—which is experienced in the five-star hotels and high rises—reveals the blatant discrimination between the rich minority Muslim Sunnis, and the poor majority Shi'ites.

It was Christmas time, and in the lobby of the hotel where we were staying, there was a gingerbread house and a giant Christmas tree. It seemed unreal to be in an Arab country, just a few miles away from Saudi Arabia, witnessing Christian festivities, with plans that evening to attend a rap concert.

Coolio delivered. We were standing in the very front, right against the stage. For the finale, Coolio walked on stage wearing a navy-blue gospel robe and began rapping the lyrics to "Gangsta's Paradise," which I knew by heart. The crowd went crazy, and halfway through the song, he pulled a couple of fans on stage, including me. I stood next to Coolio with my mouth wide open in amazement. An unforgettable, unthinkable night, in the backyard of my own country.

Bahrain was not the only Arab Gulf country we visited. Ahmed had distant relatives in Oman. Before then, I believed that Arab landscape consisted of vast dune-filled deserts and palm trees, so Oman was a stunning surprise. With striking vegetation and mountains at the edge of the seashores, it reminded me of Southern Italy, the Amalfi Coast to be exact.

Ahmed's relatives had immigrated from Mecca to Oman several decades ago and had become affiliated with both the Omani political and business scenes. The Omani family was very wealthy. While planning our trip to Oman, to my gut-wrenching surprise, Ahmed told me that, on this trip, he wanted me to wear a hijab.

I was livid. Furious. Absolutely pissed.

This was never an arrangement or agreement we discussed. I wore the abaya and veil in Saudi Arabia because it was the law, but outside of the country, I refused to cover my face or head. Only women who practiced Islamic hijab did so, but most secular, modernized Muslim women didn't. I didn't ask him why; I simply refused to consider his request. My mother, ever the diplomat, encouraged me not to overreact. She reassured me that it was not the end of the world, especially if I was still going to wear regular clothes without an abaya, just a modest scarf around my head. I couldn't believe my mother would try to reason this madness into logic.

Ahmed stood his ground, "I want to make a good impression in front of my relatives, I want to present to them my modern, yet respectful and modest Muslim wife."

"This is crazy! They left Saudi Arabia; don't you think they are used to seeing modern women not wearing a hijab?" I protested,

"What if they judge you harshly because you are half-European? What if they have already formed an opinion about you and it's not a good one? There is nothing wrong with showing your Islamic pride," he insisted.

This request came out of nowhere. I was alarmed and worried about what this meant for me and my future. I wanted to go to Oman. I saw this as an opportunity to rebel because I feared a potential pattern was unfolding. What's the worst thing that could happen? He would ultimately divorce me? After tasting freedom, I didn't really care. My pride was holding me afloat, and my unwavering desire to assert myself as a strong-willed and empowered woman was more important than anything else I could think of. Negotiations were out of the question because that would give him too much power. I decided to let it go and plotted my retaliation for the right time.

We arrived in Oman. I wore a denim dress and a scarf around my head. We checked-in at the hotel and contacted Ahmed's distant cousin, Lana. Years ago, Ahmed told me, he had a crush on Lana. I was not particularly jealous, but curious. We arrived at the family's palace which made it clear they were beyond wealthy. A butler in traditional Omani clothes, with the distinctive colorful turban, opened the door, and Lana came running to greet us. She hugged Ahmed—a very unusual, in fact, inappropriate, gesture in Arab customs—and me. She was warm and animated. She was also wearing a leather miniskirt and a tank top. Her long, dark curly hair was uncovered. I was steaming, boiling, stewing. I was pretty much overcooked in every sense of the word. I felt humiliated, insulted, irate. *This is not who I am!* Lana was meeting a meek, conservative "wifey," a totally bizarre version of me that Ahmed had fabricated.

It was lunch time, and Lana suggested we meet some of her friends at her favorite restaurant, a lively Mexican joint in downtown Muscat. "Let's carpool! I'll drive, wait at the main gate, I'll bring my car around," she said.

Within minutes, a two-door bright yellow Mercedes 300L rounded the corner of where we waited. The gullwing doors automatically opened and, as Ahmed pulled the seat forward so I could hop in the back, Lana warned abruptly, "*A'h!*" This is an all-round girl-power car, boys in the back!"

FUCK YEAH! I'm gonna like this bitch! I threw the head scarf in the back of the car next to Ahmed and fused myself to the passenger seat before buckling the seatbelt.

Rebel act number one: *check*.

My westernized husband had lived in Saudi Arabia too long. He had gone from being the carefree, liberal Americanized dude, to a professional Saudi banker, preoccupied with a culture-faith-based crisis. I was seeing the signs, but this trip opened my eyes to the impending changes that happen in a relationship, especially as growth and evolution unfold in opposite directions for each member of the twosome.

By now I figured Ahmed was disenchanted with his Omani cousin, Lana. He didn't appreciate seeing her hug and kiss all her guy friends and gulp down two margaritas during lunch. But I found myself feeling more and more comfortable around her and her wild community.

That night we received an invitation to a party hosted by one of her rich friends. We arrived at his elegant house in a lush area of the affluent neighborhood and pulled up to valet parking. As I got ready to get out of our rental car, Ahmed reminded me of my head scarf. *Are you fucking serious?* I thought, my voice screaming in my head. In a calm outer voice, I said, "No, I don't think so, but thanks for asking."

"Jasmin, I am not asking you, I am telling you," he replied, through clenched teeth.

Still keeping my infamously aggravating, sarcastic cool, I said, "Tell you what, you go to the party and when Lana asks you why I am not with you, tell her it's because you have a disobedient bitch for a wife, who is officially NOT a hijab wearer and who refuses to follow your orders and cover her head."

That was the first and last time Ahmed tried to impose his dress-code demands on me. He knew I was fully loaded and he was the perfect target. He decided his image as a man was more important than the image of his wife in a hijab. He never asked me to cover my hair after that, and I never again allowed any man to tell me what I can and can't wear.

Rebel act number two: *check.*

AMERICAN DREAMER

I grew up watching Disney's animated movies, mostly dubbed in Italian. I loved the music, the magic, and the optimism of it all. For a young Arab girl, those movies were an escape; I could pretend to be Mowgli, surrounded by animals in a wild jungle, live vicariously through Alice's odd adventures and peculiar encounters in Wonderland, or dream to be lost in Paris as were Duchess and her three artistic kittens, Berlioz, Marie, and Toulouse in the Aristocats. The lost boys in Peter Pan, so authentically themselves, encouraged me to believe in fairies and never grow up. I knew all the Disney songs, mostly in Italian, and recognized the reuse of cartoon cells from one movie to the other.

It was no surprise that when Ahmed and I finally planned our first trip to The United States, Walt Disney World was the top destination. The fourteen hour long non-stop flight from Riyadh to Orlando was made longer by my impatience and childlike anticipation. We arrived in Orlando mid-morning, checked into the Comfort Inn at Lake Buena Vista for $35 a night, thanks to the Labor Day Holiday special price back in 1994, and since our room was not ready, but the Disney shuttle was taking off, we stored our luggage in the lobby and hopped aboard, off to The Magic Kingdom. The sight of Cinderella's castle from a distance instantly took me away from the world I belonged to and catapulted me into a world I never wanted to leave.

Americans are wonderful! I thought. Everyone was happy, polite, friendly, and from what I could decipher, real lovers of life. People in the street smiled and said hello when they walked past me, something I had never really experienced before anywhere else in the world. Having no awareness that I was in a fantasy land, and certainly in a tourist-rich area, I thought all of America was like this. I wanted to stay here forever. There were so many different cultures, languages, ethnicities, races, and backgrounds around me. Why would anyone want to live anywhere else? I felt at home. My sense of belonging was reinforced by the refrain of "It's a Small World," which cycled endlessly in my brain. Before this visit, Ahmed and I had dreamed about moving to the States one day. After spending my first two hours in America, this dream became my personal goal.

I got to meet Mickey, Minnie, Donald, Daisy, Goofy, Pluto, Winnie the Pooh, Peter Pan, Captain Hook, Maleficent, Snow White, Aladdin and the REAL Princess Jasmine. It was overwhelming. If I was losing my mind, I couldn't imagine how children felt. Maybe for them it was more real and casual because their world was made of all this stuff. For me, it was an escape, an adventure of a lifetime, a fantastical world of utopia. We stood in line for hours just to ride a three-minute rollercoaster in the dark—why? Because we could— everything seemed to run on an alternate clock, in an alternate reality. It was a world ruled by the Mad Hatter: eat when you want, eat what you want, hug everyone, scream at the top of your lungs as the parade goes by, get wet on rides or in the ten-minute-afternoon-thunderstorm shower, spot as many Disney characters as you can, meet the beloved Mary Poppins and sing *Supercalifragilisticexpialidocious*, spend money—because where else would you find a t -shirt with Mickey's face for $40? (more than our nightly hotel stay)—and by golly, be merry!

Orlando swept us off our feet. We returned every year after that and, each time, spent a whole month, purchased an annual Disney pass, and somehow became part of the revolving door of the regular visitors. We made friends with some of the entertainers at the parks, in particular at Pleasure Island, the park that is no longer there, but that in the 1990's was a hub for night life to keep the party going for adults. At Pleasure Island we befriended a group of talented comedians, where each night they delivered PG improv hilarity at the Comedy Warehouse.

One of the performers there was Mary Thompson Hunt. Her comedic delivery was impeccable, her improv genius was unmatched. But she was more than that. Mary glowed from the inside out. She had a kind smile and mischievous eyes. She reminded me of my childhood, a time and place where I was not made aware of the difference in gender, race, and class. She reflected that pure time in my unjaded awareness. She was humble but strikingly educated. Mary's voice was unmarked by any accent, her features would seem familiar to every culture and ethnicity, and her warmth was that of a mother, a sister, a friend, and a neighbor.

I have met individuals in my life who seemed to be long lost friends or relatives. We have all experienced that occasional strong connection when meeting someone for the first time. Meeting Mary felt that way. My heart was happy when I was around her. She was funnier than shit, a wicked mimic, and she embodied all the greats before her. To this day her humor and beautiful voice continues to entertain visitors on Main Street at the Magic Kingdom. She became a highlight of our time in Orlando every summer, and we became friends.

Ahmed and I met Mary's husband Jason, an artist in his own right who draws realistically gorgeous black and white portraits, mostly celebrating Black Americans. He has also painted stunning U.S. landscapes, one of which he gave to me, the silhouette of a dark canyon against a moonlit night sky. That painting became a talisman, a vision board that kept my dreams alive. Mary and I remained in touch over the years, even after I stopped going to Orlando as frequently as I did back in the 1990's. When I returned to the Magic Kingdom, after exactly twenty years my reunion with Mary was a moment in time that froze everything around us. We locked in a long, tight, tearful embrace in the heart of Disney's Magic Kingdom. Mary was the catalyst of my evolving love affair with America. She transformed my tourist filter into a tangible experience of friendship that opened my eyes to a possible future. She became the ambassador who bridged the fantasy world at Disney and the real world in society.

I wanted to experience everything American. What is more American than going to the movies? I had never been in a movie theater before. My conservative culture prohibited any form of public entertainment. My first exposure was the Cadillac of theaters, the AMC at Disney Village. It was the year of *The Lion King*. I wanted my first movie theater experience to be perfect. Because I didn't know that the center of the back row is the best seat, I sat in the very front row, with my enormous Lion King bucket of popcorn. The huge screen that played the opening number, "The Circle of Life," swallowed me, and I started to cry. When the movie was over, I asked Ahmed if we could watch it again.

"I think we have to go out and buy tickets," he said.

"But what if we just stayed here, how will they know?" I replied in jest.

That month we ended up seeing *The Lion King* nine times but paid for it only once. Each time we went to the theater and bought tickets for a movie, we always snuck into *The Lion King* after watching the movie we had gone to see. It was also the year of *Forrest Gump*. It seemed as if they knew I was in America for the first time, and they wanted to make sure this new American dreamer learned U.S. history in swift Hollywood fashion, so what better class than the two hours of Forrest Gump's biography?

I yearned to be viewed as a local when I was in America. The giveaway was my nervous reaction when someone asked where we were from. I was also yanked back to my reality when I would whisper softly to Ahmed, "It would be so easy to live like this if we didn't have those goddamn *Mutawas* in our society!" Both of us would look over our shoulders for fear of being heard by the secret Saudi police which we believed existed everywhere.

Ahmed would reply, "Shh! Be careful! There are Arabs around us!"

Would we get in trouble for expressing our thoughts even if we were in America, I wondered? Was this fear rational? Everything seemed so perfect outside of Saudi Arabia. My naïve perception was certainly a manifestation of my own limited freedoms.

In my head, Walt Disney World became my adopted home; Ahmed on the other hand, yearned to go back to the home he knew growing up, Manhattan. If I thought that all of America was like Disney World, it didn't take long before I realized, it was not. New York was a huge culture shock that fascinated and intrigued me, but also overwhelmed me and left me aghast. Like Disney World, diversity-infused New York, but unlike Disney

World, New York's residents seemed eccentric, angry, self-centered, rude, loud, aggressive, aloof, and busy. If I was afraid of being mugged in Naples, I was afraid of being murdered in New York. But I remembered my Napoletano angel, and I was *not* going to stereotype an entire city just because I saw it in every movie and TV series about NY, nor would I be influenced by the loud sound of sirens that never stopped, or by the distressing yelling of mentally ill individuals who walked in traffic without a care in the world. New York was powerful, but it did little to dislodge my Disney-shaped perception of America.

Luckily, we were in good hands. We spent our ten days in New York with Ahmed's best friend. Rashon and Ahmed grew up together. His mother was Egyptian, and his father was African American, from Queens. Ahmed felt at home in New York, but Rashon *was* New York. His talk, his walk, his cues, his choices, his decisions, everything he said and did, was New York to the T. Ahmed's parents loved Rashon and his mom, who had become family over the years. While we were visiting, Ahmed's father called us one afternoon to say hello to everyone. The phone call annoyed me. I was triggered and felt harassed by the reality I wanted to flee, albeit for a short time.

One time, Rashon took us to Harlem, but only after instructing us how to behave, "People ain't gonna like it 'round here, seeing a black guy and a Puerto Rican dude, walking down the street with a young white chick." Rashon was aware that in America, Ahmed was profiled as a Latino or Puerto Rican because of his ambiguous Southeast Asian and Arab mixture. Given this, Rashon told Ahmed to turn his cap backwards, gave me gum to chew visibly, like an Italian girl from Jersey, and instructed us to ignore the swag of his walk with the limp. *What was happening?* It was the 1990's, and stereotype profiling was a way to survive. I didn't know or understand any of this, nor would it be fathomable to say it and live it in today's world.

But New York just became more interesting.

Our visit was a blend of local and tourist experiences. Overcome with emotion when I visited the Statue of Liberty, I reflected on what she represented and symbolized. As I took in the awe and promise that she has inspired in so many hopeful immigrants seeking economic prosperity, I thought *maybe one day she too will be my beacon,* as I seek social and political freedom.

Ahmed fulfilled a bucket list wish one evening when we scored a reservation at the iconic Tavern on The Green in the heart of Central Park. I fulfilled my wish by visiting The Museum of Natural History. Ever since I saw the musical, *On the Town,* with Gene Kelly, Ann Miller and Frank Sinatra, I wanted to meet the dinosaur that they destroyed in one of the movie's show stopping song-and-dance-numbers, *Prehistoric Man.* To my great disappointment, the dinosaur was a prop in the movie, and its only appearance in the museum was a tiny homage picture on the wall of the gift shop.

Rashon was responsible for our local experiences, and one morning he took us to Barnes and Noble on Fifth Avenue, where he was ecstatic to meet a famous football player who was there for a book signing. After hours in a line that wrapped around two blocks, we met a soft spoken, shy, not so tall but super buff guy named Emmitt Smith. It wasn't until years later that I grasp what a big deal that the short, shy, buff guy was.

Perhaps the most New York thing I experienced was going to Broadway shows. We saw several over the years, including *Something Happened on The Way to The Forum,* with Nathan Lane, but nothing on a stage will ever compare to the moment I finally saw Dame Julie Andrews. This was the last season she was performing in *Victor Victoria,* and the show was almost sold out. I didn't just want to go to the show, I wanted front row seats. Ahmed and I stopped by the lobby of the Marriott where the show was playing and asked for the best seats in the house for that night. "Hmm it looks like someone just cancelled two front row seats; would you like them?" asked the box office attendant.

Do I scream? Do I faint? I played it cool. "Sure, we'll take them," I said, casually, knowing we were most likely going to have to skip dinner to afford the tickets.

I had repeatedly watched *The Sound of Music,* more than any other movie in my life. I not only know all the songs but can recite every spoken word in it. At every age in my life, I have used it as a therapeutic escape, sometimes watching the three-hour movie twice in a day—when you grow up in a socially reserved and depriving culture, you have plenty of time on your hands. Julie's performance as Fräulein Maria put her on the level of goddess in my book, and I still have her glowing on my feminist pedestal. She followed her dreams. Fräulein Maria did not fit in at the convent but did not allow that detail to change who she was or dampen her passions. I looked up to her. She was perfect. She was hope. Christopher Plummer as Captain Von Trapp was my first crush, and at six years old I believed I would marry him one day. I wanted to be one of the Von Trapps. The charm of the era and the horrors of WWII mesmerized me. I felt a familiarity with the theme of nuns, a reminder of my family's Catholic Italian heritage. But most of all, I loved the music, which was a healing tool through the hardest of times.

When Julie Andrews performed the last outrageous number of her Broadway musical—playing a woman pretending to be a man in drag—she was three feet away from the edge of the stage, where I sat. I looked straight into her eyes, smiled, and waved, begging for her acknowledgment, the same longing carried over since my teens. She smiled back, winked, and blew me a kiss, sealing my belief in dreaming big.

Each year that we returned to America, I had a chance to see it more realistically. By the second year, some of the more obviously imperfect aspects of the American life tempered my adoration of the country. The first visit succeeded because of our frugal spending. We used all our money on the Theme Park tickets and entertainment, but for food we shopped at the local Walgreens for a loaf of Wonder Bread and several cans of tuna and a jar of mayonnaise. Tuna sandwiches, for lunch and dinner, hostess cupcakes for breakfast. It's so easy and cheap to eat in America!

After four weeks of sustaining ourselves on that wallet-appealing diet, we felt sick. For the two of us, who grew up on wholesome, unprocessed, home-cooked meals, suddenly the short cut was no longer an option. The following year, we decided to use the coupon booklets, and went to fast food joints where they offered two-for-one meals that included more than three ingredients. Sure, Long John Silver's and McDonald's were a step up from the makeshift Walgreen's deli sandwich we slapped together, but this time it only took one week before I was done with fried food-like things. That's when we decided to upgrade and explore The Olive Garden and Red Lobster.

OK, maybe now I'm starting to see that not EVERYTHING about America is perfect. Fair enough, it can't ALL be perfect, but that's ok, because ... Disney World!

My ability to see imperfections did not stop at New York City's madness or at Orlando's pharmacy meals and fast-food joints, because my next experience was Walmart. At first glance, this place looked like the Walt Disney World for *frugal-ites.* Everything under one roof, at "Always Low Prices"—heck it's in their slogan—but I may be one of few to have had an immediate aversion. The florescent lights, the smell of plastic, the messy shelves and unhappy employees walking around in blue vests that seemed to mock the customers with the question stenciled on the back, "How May I Help You?" Walmart was nothing to write home about, which is to say that America was not perfect. But was I really going to compare the silly quirks of fast-food cuisine, big corporations and chaotic cities with oppression, oppression, and oppression?

Unwavering. I still had my heart set on this American life.

OPRAH WINFREY

The first time I heard of Oprah Winfrey was on an episode of the 80s sitcom, *Silver Spoons*. In the episode, the main character, Edward—Ricky's dad—finds out that his ex-wife had written a novel about a woman's turbulent relationship with a man. He believed the character in the novel was based on him. Edward loses sleep over the fact that his dirty laundry may have been aired out in this new book. What little sleep he gets he ends up having a crazy dream in which he and his ex-wife are on *The Oprah Winfrey Show* discussing the details of their relationship. Oprah—played ironically by his housekeeper, Jo Marie—is a dynamic and strong woman who boasts striking interviewing skills.

I wasn't sure if Oprah was a real person based on an actual talk show. Her name alone, odd as it sounded, made me wonder, but from the audience's reaction to that scene, my guess was, perhaps she was.

By the mid-1990's, thanks to the changes that came about after the Gulf War of '91 and the presence of U.S. troops in the Kingdom, almost every house had sprouted a satellite dish on the roof, turning the desert cities into a harvest of metal mushrooms. I gravitated towards the music channels, and watched the latest music videos by Michael Jackson, MC Hammer, Oasis, Spice Girls, No Doubt, and The Fugees. I also became hooked on *Beverley Hills 90210*, and each week was eager to see what Tori Spelling was wearing and, of course, swooned over Luke Perry.

Flipping through the many channels one morning, I came across a talk show, where I saw a gorgeous woman in red with short dark hair and a smile that filled the screen. She was holding a microphone and talking to a large, captivated audience. I paused for a second and listened. This woman was an orator, she was smart, inspiring, and compassionate. At that point in my life, I was not very interested in talk shows. During my first trip to the U.S. I had binged on Jerry Springer, Sally Jesse Raphael and Geraldo—for three nights in a row. I was over-saturated with the circus that unfolded on these talk shows. In fact, I even attended a live taping of the Sally Jesse Raphael show in New York, and got confirmation that it is all an act, especially when I was pulled out of the audience and questioned by security, after they noticed my fancy Minolta camera. They asked me if I was from the *National Enquirer*.

This show was different. It was not a voyeuristic spectacle, but more like therapy. I did not know what I was watching, or who, until the commercial break when an announcer intoned, "Next, on Oprah..." I didn't hear anything else he said after that; the name Oprah stopped me in my tracks.

OH MY GOD! It's the REAL Oprah!

By now I was hooked on *The Oprah Winfrey Show*. I watched it religiously. No other show on TV mattered. I had no faith-based community, and I did not belong to a mosque, because women are peripheral to religious institutions and because I was never interested in such a community. Oprah became my pastor, and her sermons were what I longed for every single day.

I wanted to know everything about Oprah, where she came from, how she became—what I now realized was—the most successful woman in television history. Who was she, and what was it about her that made her such a captivating figure? I searched and researched, but I could not find an autobiography in my local bookstores. The following summer, at a Barnes and Noble in Orlando, I found *Oprah Winfrey – The Definitive Story of Her Struggle and Success* by George Mair, a paperback book of about 370 pages. I read that book in two days, and after I was done, I read it again, cover to cover. I kept the book by my bed, where I found something comforting about having Oprah next to me, reminding me of my own struggles and strengths. She was a female figure whom I could look up to and hold onto for inspiration and for a miraculous change.

I read about her painful childhood, how she came into the world unplanned and unwanted by her parents who had a one-night stand. I found out that her grandmother raised her as a child. A housemaid for a white family, she told Oprah to watch carefully as she hung wet clothes on the line and to learn how to do this job well, because one day, she too will find *some nice white folks* to work for. Even as a young five-year-old, Oprah knew she would not hang wet clothes on a line for *nice white folks.* Oprah was determined from a very young age to better herself and escape the environment in which she was raised. She had her trials, troubles, and tribulations, but she never wavered on her goal; she wanted to be of help to others, and when she realized she had what it takes, she wanted to be of service to the world.

If Oprah could do it, so could any woman, so could I.

I wasn't seeking her lifestyle, her fame or notoriety; rather, I sought her confidence, her freedom, and her determination.

Obsessed with Oprah's message, I watched as she helped women see their own strengths. Women who escaped abusive relationships, women who overcame horrific childhoods, women who liberated themselves from harsh conditions to make something of themselves. She told stories of women from other countries, who found the courage and determination to succeed thanks to education. She had guests who overcame the worst adversities, from racial discrimination to sexual abuse, from injustices and cruelties to self-loathing. Oprah aired it all out. She brought these topics to the surface and armed every single one of her audience members with the hope and tools to do the same. She created a platform that showcased experts in the fields of recovery and motivation. When she had famous people and celebrities on her show they served a purpose to inspire, without a money-making voyeuristic interest in their lives.

Oprah was a teacher, a healer, and a true mentor.

I kept my obsession with Oprah at bay, not wanting to draw attention to her influence, because I feared she'd be taken away from me somehow, like Michael Jackson had been. Oprah was dangerous; she was a threat that could awaken docile women. In fact, most women around me who watched Oprah seemed to be more interested in her make-over tips, the interviews with celebrities, and her extravagant giveaways. I was glad that her message of empowerment went unnoticed in my world. I hoped that if there were other women listening to her like I was, they too chose to be discreet and subtle. If we were to take her advice to heart, we needed to do it without attracting much scrutiny from those who thus far had power over us.

I had all the ingredients needed to build a revolution within me. As Oprah encouraged her audience to reflect on their own childhood and their own barriers, she shed light on how those great lessons can serve as fuel for a drastic shift and change. Oprah reiterated in many of her shows, "The biggest adventure you can ever take is to live the life of your dreams." I accepted her invitation and evaluated my own childhood that had unfolded not long ago, examining all the challenges that had the possibility to serve me or hold me hostage.

My life was not horrible like some of the women she interviewed on her show. I was never imprisoned, physically abused, raped, mentally harmed, or starving. I had a loving family, a safe upbringing with several privileges that afforded me happy experiences. So why did I feel so compelled to react to her message?

I began to understand my fears, worries, and anxieties. We are wired to be productive, to be seen and heard. While my life was in no immediate and physical danger, my existence felt like it was. My purpose was under threat. If I didn't have personal freedom of expression, I wouldn't reach my highest potential. I would never find out what my purpose is. There was an urgency to unshackle my innermost self, my worth, my value. All that had been taken from me, I now realized, had been stripped away without my consent. The message I heard from Oprah loud and clear was: only I had the power to define my destiny. That, however, was not the message told to me from birth, nor was it the life offered me as a Saudi Arabian woman. I had dwelled on *why was I born here?* most of my life, but my energies had now shifted to *what can I do to take my power back, how can I use my life to find meaning?* Oprah offered that hope, and I became an eager apprentice in training.

On occasion, Oprah's name came up in social situations. I always noticed the men's uncomfortable reactions, their body language and their words seeming to show an aversion and disapproval of this powerful woman. Oprah came up one time when we were with a group of friends who, like us, were all young childless couples, most of the men Saudi or Arab, the wives, a mixed batch. When one of the wives commented on an Oprah show, her husband jumped in before she could finish, and said "Oh, please! Not Oprah again, the woman is an angry bitch, she's a man-hater with major issues. I mean, she's black, she's fat, she can't be all that happy, she's probably a lesbian, why is she telling us how to live our lives?!"

Most of the men chuckled and laughed, but his wife—who must have known she was married to a dick—waved her hand at him as if to say *oh whatever!* and continued talking to me about a kitchen gadget she had seen on the show. I had a hard time following her enthusiasm and an even harder time withholding my desire to slap her husband.

Instead, I simply said, "Is Oprah a threat to you?"

"WHAT?! Of course not," he laughed.

"Then why did you need to attack her so viciously? She's not even here!"

"That's my opinion of her, in fact, it's probably the opinion of many."

"Perhaps. And perhaps it would be best if she kept to herself, and knew where her place is, like every woman should. Am I right?" I asked sarcastically.

"Hey! I'm not a sexist—"

Before he could finish, I interrupted and said, "Oh, no, not at all. You just seem to have very formed, descriptive, racist, gender-based, hostile, homophobic, and provoked opinions of this woman. How do you feel about Phil Donahue? Larry King? Carson?—pick one."

"Pfft! I don't have an opinion about that!"

Case Closed.

In contrast to that group of friends was a couple we befriended in Riyadh and socialized with briefly before they left to go back to their home in Pennsylvania. Hoda was from Egypt and educated in the States, where she met her American husband Tim, the only western man in our circle. They had been married for ten years and had two beautiful little girls. They didn't get to do a lot of things as a couple because their jobs and their children demanded their focus. They lived in an American compound where they enjoyed the many perks of American life: no abaya, playgrounds, public swimming pool, mini movie-theaters, and baseball fields. Both Hoda and Tim worked as computer engineers for U.S. companies in Riyadh. They occasionally hosted barbecues and movie nights.

Ahmed and I attended one of their movie nights just weeks before they left. I remember it was a large group of people, folks we didn't know, most of them Westerners, and Hoda and I were the only two Arab women. The movie, *Heat*, with De Niro and Pacino, was holding everyone's attention, except for mine. Even though I loved both De Niro and Pacino, my attention was focused on something far more pulling.

I watched Tim and Hoda cuddled on the floor eating popcorn, taking turns to check on the kids, or console one of them when they would make their way out of the bedroom and into the living room because they couldn't sleep. The loving interaction between Hoda and Tim, and the awe-inducing interaction between Tim and his children had my mind captivated in admiration and envy. I wanted what they had. I wanted what Hoda had. She was an Arab woman married to a Western man, so, it was possible. That was the first time that I admitted to myself that I wished I too could have a Western husband. I never wanted to marry a Saudi man. As time went by and Ahmed became more ingrained in Saudi culture and society, he was less of the westernized husband I needed, and more of the husband I avoided.

Just weeks after visiting Hoda and Tim's home, I saw an episode on Oprah about successful marriages and relationships, and I started to wonder how much longer I could go on in a situation that I knew was not meant for the long haul.

We all deserve to live the life we want. We all have the power to make that life happen.

This was the message I got from Oprah, and from Louise Hay, the new age guru whose books my mother had introduced me to. Louise reinforced my inner peace and positive attitude, the one that said, "I am in the right place, at the right time, doing the right thing," but Oprah reinforced my warrior spirit and rebel attitude, the one that said, "It doesn't matter who you are or where you come from. The ability to triumph begins with you—always."

Louise Hay continued to be a wonderful soul companion, and a trusted guru. I got through some tumultuous times with her teachings and philosophy. After losing Nebras to cancer and Lamia in a car accident, I thought grief would be the only emotion I would ever feel. I assumed healing was only for cuts and scrapes, and not the heart. But Louise changed my perception, with her own story and the many others that she shared of people's grief and healing. Now that I stood stronger and in recovery from the pain and the grief of my adolescence, I was ready to move forward, and this time, Oprah had the answers. She armed me with the greatest weapon of all, my mind. The force of Oprah empowered me. I became the author of my life, able to identify and draw significance from life events.

In my darkest of times, I had Louise Hay, my New Age muse, who gave me the tools and the manual on how to do the work in order to have the clout and authority to stand on my own two feet.

In my teens I had Mary Boissel, my English teacher from Ireland, who made me believe in myself and helped me see how truly smart I was. She opened my mind to the possibility of thinking outside of the box and exercise my views on social and global realties.

In my twenties I had Oprah Winfrey, my intellectual hero on satellite TV, who made me believe in hope, and reinforced the message of birthright. Oprah pointed my attention towards the undeniable place I had in this world and what I had to do to claim that space. If I was told time and time again by the environment that surrounded me that I was dispensable, Oprah firmly helped me see how worthy I was.

VALENTINO

Oprah's two beloved cocker spaniels, Sophie and Solomon, became household names. Her relationship with her dogs affirmed my long-held and forlorn desire to have a dog of my own. Having a dog would fill a void and symbolize my impatient fantasy of asserting my independence. It would also buy me time to escape the pressures of having a child.

There was a pet store in downtown Riyadh where I often went. The owner, Dr. Ma'moon, was an eccentric and friendly Palestinian man. He was a vet with a clear love for animals, but short on social skills with humans. He lacked healthy boundaries, especially in the reserved Saudi culture. I never took offense at his bizarre stories—like the one he told of the cat that was brought into his clinic after a horrid man had sexually violated the poor animal—or his failure to respect personal space by getting too close to my face when he spoke to me. It seemed as though he had no problem connecting with animals, and the love was visibly mutual.

During one of my many visits to that pet shop—where I usually got to hold exotic animals or interacted with the many cats they had for sale—a gentle tap on my shoulder startled me; when I turned around, I saw Dr. Ma'moon holding a black and gray long-haired mutt with smart eyes and paws almost clasped. The creature looked straight into my eyes while its little curly tail wagged in supersonic speed. I grabbed the little guy and held him close under my chin, both of us lovingly melting into each other. Dr. Ma'moon knew of my weakness for dogs, and he played this introduction perfectly.

I looked at Ahmed and said, "I need this puppy!! I want this puppy!"

He replied in a compassionate voice, "Well, you know the money we saved up is for our summer trip to Orlando, do you want the dog or the trip?"

I sensed his hesitation. The obstacles he rationally observed in that moment were the financial burden, but also his family's cultural practices towards dogs and their place in the home. I, on the other hand, was *this much* closer to fulfilling a childhood dream.

"I want both! I will sell my gold and get enough money to buy the dog," I said without pause.

Dr. Ma'moon agreed to hold the dog for a couple of days for me, and in less than twenty-four hours, I had sold most of the gold I owned and made 4,000 riyals (about $750) to buy that pup.

This was my first dog, and I was jumping out of my skin with excitement. I couldn't believe that, this time, I was bringing home a real, live, moving, barking, breathing dog. Within seconds, all my previous stuffed and invisible pets flashed through my mind, and I wondered if this moment was a mystic manifestation, the great *law of attraction,* after years of visualizing myself as a dog mom.

At the pet shop, I bought a red collar, leash, bed, toys, treats, and food. In the car on the ride home, I held the puppy in my lap, trying hard to come up with the perfect name for him. When I fantasized of this day since childhood, I had a million names ready, but when this little guy came into my life so unexpectedly, none seemed to fit, and I believed he would choose his name in the most unpredictable way. I knew no matter what, I wanted an Italian name, I wanted a sweet name. Driving through the fancy district in Riyadh on the way home, we passed the Valentino store. I exclaimed "*Valentino!*" and the little pup looked up at me and wagged his tail. Sooner than I imagined, we had found his name.

Valentino lived up to his name. He was a lover, a true valentine. He was affectionate, and well-mannered. Bringing Valentino home was thrilling, but once it all sank in, I realized I was going to be faced with several challenges as well. We lived in an apartment on the twelfth floor; potty training him was going to be tricky. It was not possible for me to walk him anywhere during the night or day. Not only was it taboo to own a dog, but it was also not safe or acceptable for a woman to walk in the neighborhood—let alone with a dog—so I had to find a way to get him potty trained indoors. There was an unfurnished room in our apartment, meant to be used as a second living room for the option to *gender-segregate* guests as is the cultural norm, which we didn't need or use. It was an uncarpeted room and we reserved it for storage. I laid out newspapers for Valentino, and within a couple of days he was fully potty trained.

The other challenge was society as a whole and Ahmed's family in particular. Dogs were not raised as pets in Saudi Arabia. Since they were viewed as filthy animals, many Muslims choose not to enter homes where dogs live, and I realized quickly this was the case with Ahmed's family. I knew that the dog would create a chasm between us and his parents, a thought I entertained with private delight. In the years that we lived in that apartment with Valentino, Ahmed's family visited our home only three times, making sure the dog was contained to his potty room. While Valentino was not welcome in their home, I took him to my parent's house every time I visited. My father was smitten and worked very hard at teaching him tricks, failing miserably at the command to *shake*. *"Dammi la manina!"* he would repeat patiently while Valentino panted gleefully and staring at him adoringly. Even so, my father was not discouraged, and was happy with the thrill of trying. My siblings treated Valentino like a little nephew, and even my mom grew to affectionately tolerate his many visits.

Valentino was bilingual, but Italian was his first language. He understood all commands in Italian, and a few in English. He bonded with my parents and siblings, and when Ahmed and I went on vacation, he stayed at my parents' home.

It wasn't long before I made up dozens of love names for Valentino, Mr T, Tee Tee, Tea bag, and Mr. Buff Buff (after his muffled bark). To all, however, he was known as Tino, the name to which he most enthusiastically responded. Tino exceeded all the expectations I had about being a dog mom. It took months for me to realize this was not a dream. Everything happened so fast, and the reality of finally having a pet dog continued to seem like a fantasy.

Tino grew to be about twenty-five pounds. He was strong and gentle. He was long haired with bangs that covered his eyes, he had perky ears that were always on alert, and a long pink tongue that often dangled out the side of his mouth. Tino wore his red leather collar with a blue bone shaped name tag. He was not allowed on our bed or in our bedroom; Ahmed wanted a clean and dog-free space for praying. Every morning when Ahmed opened the bedroom door and went into the bathroom, Tino would quietly run into our bedroom, perch himself on my side of the bed to say good morning, before I kissed him and told him to go wait for me outside. Tino was a perfect companion. He sat in my lap when we watched TV and snuggled when I lay on the couch to read. He stood in my lap in the car while he poked his head out the window. He was by my side when I was in the kitchen, hoping for accidental crumbs to drop on the floor. He loved curling up by my feet when I was at my keyboard playing, composing, or recording music. I wrote several songs for him, including one to the tune of Alanis Morissette's 1990's hit, "Ironic," that my sister May and I still sing.

When I travelled to the U.S. every summer, I shopped at the same local Pet Store in Lake Buena Vista in Orlando. Tino had some favorite treats that I could only find in the U.S., and of course I had to bring home tons of gifts to soothe his separation anxiety. He handled the parting better each time I left him with my family. May was his primary guardian, and he loved being with her. He was used to being at home alone during the day because both Ahmed and I worked, so he adjusted to May's work schedule as well.

In the evenings, however, he shadowed her around the house and felt reassured with her by his side. One evening when May got home after a rare occasion of visiting friends, she found a rather spectacular surprise that Tino had created for her. She wasn't sure if he was playing out his frustration and disapproval of her leaving him that evening, or if he was trying to please her as a way to say *I'm so happy you're back, please don't leave me again.* May walked into the main hall of the home and found that Tino had gathered every shoe in the house that he could get a hold of, placed them in a huge pile all together, and surrounded the pile of shoes with a ring of tissues that he pulled out of a tissue box in the family room.

Tino taught me how to love unconditionally. He was my first dog, and since then, I have always had a dog in my life. All my dogs have been loving companions, and they have each carved a very special place in my heart, but Tino was the first to crack my heart wide open, the first to affirm my childhood dream of bonding with an animal. He possessed the intelligence of a precocious child, and the heart of a wise monk. I marveled at the fact that dogs can forgive and forget so effortlessly. When I scolded him, his eyes poured out the sincerest apology, while his partial smile begged for love. He communicated in ways that no human was able to replicate. He lived to please me. Until that point, I couldn't imagine being worthy of this kind of undying devotional adoration from anyone.

WORKING WOMAN

My time at King Saud University was short lived because I struggled with the rigid, limiting social and intellectual environment. I was committed to the idea of completing my education but felt discouraged with the limited opportunities I was offered as a woman. Ahmed and I had talked about a future life in the West, and when we got married, I left the university. I held onto the idea of belonging to a liberal arts college one day, where I could pursue personal and professional ambitions without any restriction.

Soon after putting my higher education goals on hold, I turned my linguistic skills into a professional advantage and aimed for a working career as an ESL (English as a Second Language) teacher. A small, private international school hired me as an English teacher. A young Saudi woman and a charismatic America woman married to a Saudi man owned the school. These two individuals could not have been more different.

Kim, the American, was independent, strong, assertive and a highly qualified professional. Nawal, Kim's Saudi business partner, was diplomatic, wealthy, fairly educated, and culturally savvy. Kim had what it took to run a growing business, while Nawal had what it took to be a politician, a skill she needed in a school that pushed the progressive boundaries while upholding cultural and religious standards. They were a good team and working with them excited me.

Nawal had high hopes for me. As the only Saudi teacher in the school, she often hinted at the opportunity I had to rapidly grow professionally there. I felt that my language skills and citizenship mattered more to them than a degree. Kim was thrilled at the idea of working with a half-Western, half-Arab woman. She had two young daughters herself and, seeking solace for the worries she had for her girls, she asked me about how I had coped growing up.

We shared many inspiring conversations. I spoke openly about the struggles I had with my loving and progressive parents—parents who also felt the pressure of this deeply conservative society, posing unreasonable restrictions on me—and she, as an American woman married to a liberal Saudi man, spoke of dreams for her little girls who were born immediately before and after the Gulf War of '91, during which Saudi society changed in the presence of American and European troops. She hoped they would be independent women and future contributors to the Kingdom's promising progress.

Another colleague I worked with closely was Michelle, an American woman also married to a Saudi man. Michelle and I had become close friends; she was my mentor and we worked closely on lesson plans, developing the school's ESL curriculum. While she was a generation older than I, and had three sons, our difference in age and experience did not seem to affect our strong and natural connection. Michelle was from Pittsburg, an American of Italian heritage. She and I had more than cultural ties; we were both independent thinkers, and assertive women. We loved to laugh, but also spent long hours on the phone talking about deeper issues that faced us as working women in a culture that limited our freedom of expression and suppressed our intellectual curiosity. I leaned on Michelle as a colleague and as a modern woman I could look up to. I didn't know it at the time, but my subconscious was safely finding its way to my truth through this effortless and genuine friendship.

Teaching, as it turned out, was second nature for me. I come from a line of teachers: my mother was a career teacher; both my maternal grandparents and aunt were career teachers; and my father taught in his early adulthood. I felt at home in front of a classroom where I established a few firm and clear rules, but with a lot of playful tricks to aid in the success of accomplishing the goals I set out for my students. When I applied for the job,

I told them I wished to be introduced as an English teacher who only spoke English. I didn't want my young students to know I spoke Arabic because this would force them to communicate with me in English.

When students asked to go to the bathroom in Arabic, I responded "Bathroom?" in English.

"Yes!" The student would say exuberantly,

"Say bathroom, please!" I would affirm, and they would repeat without any problem.

The next time that same child would need to use the bathroom, they would raise their hand and ask confidently, "Teacher! Bathroom please?!"

Not too long before my teaching career began, I had been a young student myself. I thought often of Mrs. Boissel, and how important she had been in my own growth and education. I couldn't channel her as the ship captain that she was, because that was not my style, but I certainly drew inspiration from her powerful ability to connect with her students and exhibit investment in each of those earnest young minds.

A young, tremendously bright girl named Hana became one of my favorite students. On the first day of class I asked her, "How are you?"

She smiled wide, nodded enthusiastically, and said, "YES! Hana!"

What she lacked in linguistic knowledge, she made up for in eagerness to learn. By the end of that first year, Hana could speak English in full sentences. Her parents told me she had become the translator at home between their English-speaking Filipino help and the rest of the family.

Still a child myself, if not in body, certainly at heart, I loved the same things my students did: Disney movies, reading stories, playing music, and playing with arts and crafts. It was the early nineties, and *Aladdin* was the biggest Disney movie of the time. My little first graders told everyone in the school that their teacher was Princess Jasmine. I wore my hair in a long, pinched ponytail like the Disney princess, and the little girls and boys rushed to sit by my side during circle time so they could play with my hair while I read them stories.

I had secretly wished I could be one of the Disney characters in the theme parks; it seemed like it would be great fun to be Goofy or Minnie for a living. Alas, instead, I sometimes jumped into the large Barney costume we had at the school, despite my aversion to the creepy purple dinosaur, while my petite colleague Suraya, wore the costume of BJ, Barney's yellow sidekick. We walked around the school during lunch breaks and recess, making the kids feel loved, sharing hugs and singing the "I Love You" song.

As a teacher, I used an American curriculum by Scott Foresman that Kim, our director, had selected. It impressed me how fast my students went through the program. In fact, I had to find creative ways to expand each unit in order to extend the syllabus to the end of the academic year—a thrilling challenge because I was given the green light to be as creative and as innovative as possible. Several times a week I brought my keyboard to the classroom and taught my students songs that I wrote about the unit we were working on. When we studied the unit on animals, I brought my dog, Valentino, to school. Not only my students, but all the other students in our small school, got to meet Valentino and learn the names of his body parts in English—this would not have happened in any other Saudi school.

Within a couple of years, the school promoted me and Michelle to head English Teachers. As the youngest teacher in the school, I took my job very seriously. Thanks to Michelle's mentorship, I was now mentoring and training new teachers, and eventually had a teaching assistant (TA) assigned to me to help with worksheets and craft prepping.

My TA was Michi, a Japanese woman married to a Saudi man. Meeting Michi reminded me of my culturally diverse childhood. She spoke perfect English with a gentle Japanese accent. She had gone to school in the States where she met her Saudi husband, who had attended business school. Theirs was a union that went against cultural norms, and Michi conformed to her husband's demands, including segregating from men, covering her face in public, and following the Islamic code of conduct.

I was fascinated by the society, the culture, and the struggles of the great Japanese civilization. Everything I knew about Japan, besides Anime, electronic gadgets and cars, I had learned from one of my favorite tv shows, a Japanese soap-opera, *Oshin*, about a young Geisha's life, which Saudi censors had changed to the story of a "hairdresser." Decades later, I read the captivating graphic novel *Persepolis* by Iranian born author Marjane Satrapi, who had also watched the censored version of *Oshin* growing up in Tehran. In spite of the fact that the author and I hailed from neighboring countries that remain enemies, we had experienced astonishingly similar childhoods. Ms. Satrapi also smuggled posters and music cassettes into her country.

A couple of weeks after I started working with Michi, I realized that not only did we live in the same building, but her apartment was directly above mine. Michi's very conservative husband conducted himself in a reserved and respectful manner, and he politely turned down my attempt to introduce Ahmed to him with the proposal to socialize as couples.

This didn't stop Michi and me from becoming good friends. On the weekends, when both our husbands worked, she and I would meet at one of our apartments and cook together. Ahmed had introduced me to Japanese food, his favorite cuisine. Our first legal date in public was at the Hyatt Regency's Japanese restaurant in Riyadh. Michi and I had a great arrangement; she wanted to learn how to cook Italian food, and in exchange, she taught me how to make sushi. "Sushi is easy to make if you make the rice good. Sticky, but not too sticky," She explained. Having learned from a native, my sushi-making skills are still strong today, and I often make about 100 pieces of vegetarian sushi rolls for my family on New Year's Day. Michi worked with me at the school for a year, after which she dedicated herself to IVF treatments. She and I remained friends, and I was extremely happy for her and her husband when they finally welcomed their sweet little boy the following year.

New teachers joined the school frequently as we expanded grades and classrooms. When I joined the school, it was a kindergarten only, with clear plans to grow into a full elementary school within five years. My guarantee that I would hold the position of head teacher meant that I became a supervisor as well, and I moved up a grade each year to stay with the same group of students I had started with in first grade. I loved the idea of teaching the same cohort year after year; we bonded and became invested in one another.

Towards the end of first grade, my students put on a show for the rest of the school, and they sang the song "Under My Hat" that I had written for them from the same title of the book we had studied all year:

Here in my school, I learn many things
I can draw pictures and I can sing
I can do this and I can do that
There's someone special under my hat
Watch and you'll see, maybe you'll find
That I am one of a kind

When I composed the music that I played on the keyboard while their sweet voices sang the lyrics I wrote, I had no idea it would sound so good. My boss, Kim, teared up as she watched the kids sway and sing, holding different hats in their hands, and placing them proudly on their heads during the middle verse. Kim loved it so much, especially because her daughter, Tala, was in my class and the lead singer of the song.

Kim, impressed with our production, invited the representative from Scott Foresman to attend the school party the following week and hear my class sing the song. Patty, an American woman, and a lovely grandma-like person, worked as the rep for the Scott Foresman curriculum. After hearing my students sing, she pulled me aside and said, "This song is absolutely wonderful. I'd like to talk to you about buying the rights to it and including it in our program."

I thanked her after a few days of thinking about the proposal but turned down the offer; I was not able to assertively advocate for myself and my work, and she respectfully understood that. After hearing my kids sing that day, Patty wanted to come to our classroom and chat with them. The children gathered in their usual circle formation on the *magic carpet,* and Patty joined them, but sat on a chair because her "old joints can't take the floor," as she put it.

Patty introduced herself, and while making eye contact with each of the students she said, "I am so impressed with the work you all have done this year! I work for the company that wrote your schoolbooks, and I want you to know, I have never seen these books come to life like I did when I watched you all sing and dance!"

The students smiled in delight and pride.

"Do you have questions for me?" Patty asked, inviting the kids to interact with her in an intimate and warm way, perhaps as a way to test their English.

Hana, who by now spoke full sentences in English, could not find the words *in English* to ask her burning question. She yelled it out in Arabic, with her characteristic wide, dimply smile. After she asked the question, which naturally I understood, I noticed all the other kids whispered in agreement, repeating the same question.

Patty looked at me, asking for a translation, but I hesitated, as I found the question rather inappropriate. "Well, it's a, umm, not a school-related question, maybe we should see if someone else has a question about the books," I said to Patty and the kids.

"No, no, they can ask any questions! I am happy to answer them!" Patty said with her loud and cheerful voice, "Please translate their questions, word for word!"

"Well, umm, they want to know why you are .... uhh ... so .... *Big,*" I answered, painfully embarrassed.

"OH!" she exclaimed looking at the kids, "You want to know why I am *fat*?!" Patty said confidently and joyfully, "It's because I love to eat!"

Hana had been a wonderful, eager, and hardworking student all year, but on that day, she became the teacher, and I the student. I learned that children speak their mind and say what they mean. They don't judge others but seek an understanding if they are perplexed. I learned that true knowledge and growth comes from having the courage to ask and leave nothing unanswered. When Patty told them she loved to eat, they all saw that they had more in common with the large, blonde, blue-eyed foreigner than they thought.

"*Yes!* I like chocolate!" said one kid.

"I like pizza!" said Hana.

I finally joined in, "I like sushi!"

As is the case in most small businesses, constant changes and adjustments occurred. Some made me unhappy, while I championed others. I began sensing loyalty and politics developing within the school's administration. One day, Nawal called me into her office, and the school principal joined us. They both met me with enthusiasm, but my stomach knotted because the attention I often received from them made me uncomfortable. They informed me of their goal to have Saudi women in all the important supervising roles at the school. They wanted to promote and encourage young ambitious Saudi women and replace all the other employees in leadership roles. This included Kim, the partial owner and director of the English Department. In sworn secrecy, they verbally promised me Kim's position of department director—in the near future. Although I celebrated the idea of Saudi women moving forward in every way, I was taken aback by the offer. I was uncomfortable for many reasons, but I knew I had to display grace and gratitude.

A week later, they asked if I had given any thought about taking over the department. I told them that I could not betray Kim and that I was in no hurry to move up the ladder. The administration reacted unprofessionally to my response, rejecting my request for a deserved and promised raise, as well as withholding my annual bonus. They could not believe that I would be loyal to a Westerner—not realizing that my loyalty was to humanity, and not on the basis of nationality—and thus shatter their dream of turning the school into a glorified statistic during a time when growing pressure existed to *Saudize* jobs, businesses, and leadership positions, especially for women. I became aware of the fact that the administration operated in a self-serving way, even if it meant backstabbing some of their finest and most dedicated assets.

Their tone changed with me, and they began treating me like another non-Saudi employee whom they undervalued and underestimated.

I came to school one day after those uncomfortable and ugly negotiations wearing a *Lion King* t-shirt. My kids, who always responded to my Disney fashion and memorabilia with enthusiasm, loved the picture, but the administration, felt differently. That same day they sent a memo banning clothing with writing on it. My shirt, undoubtedly, inspired their decision. I was ok with it, because after all, I got to make my statement. The front of my shirt had a picture of the evil lion Scar standing in the middle of his loyal hyenas; on the back of the shirt, what I knew the children could not yet read, the infamous line that Scar mutters, "I'm surrounded by idiots."

PROFESSIONAL WOMAN

I thought I had found my purpose and calling in life. Being a teacher was a gratifying and rewarding job. However, it wasn't long after the awkward interactions with the school administration that I reached the burdening conclusion that I was at risk of losing my strong stance on educational and social ethics.

The school system was proving to be a political bureaucratic structure that calculated ways to control society for personal—as well as corporate—profit. I saw clearly how the public-school system utilized its non-profit status to tactfully impose a belief system that produced the kind of citizens that served the higher purpose of society. In contrast, private schools lured the intellectually hungry folks into a more progressive and liberal model that was nothing more than a brilliantly orchestrated ploy, masked by the fancy buildings and token appearance of the arts, to deliver the same message of conformity that was instituted in the public-school system—all for a lucrative profit.

It soon became clear that my unwillingness to play the game according to the unspoken rules of the establishment greatly challenged my professional aspirations. After four years, I decided the time had come to leave my desk, my classroom, my colleagues and my students. A couple of years before I left, my dear colleague Michelle had quit for similar reasons of discontent with how favoritism and politics interfered with our ability to perform our demanding jobs. After Michelle left the school, she found a position as an English teacher at another international, diplomatic school where she was respected and appreciated for her fine-tuned skills and long experience. When I decided to leave too, Michelle supported me with great empathy and encouragement.

Because I could be myself with Michelle, I didn't censor my words or keep my dreams private. I shared my personal frustrations and confided in her my wish to break free. Like me, she was married to a Saudi. Like my mother, she was a Western mother to half-Saudi kids. But unlike me, she knew what it was like to grow up with total freedom; and unlike my mother, she didn't choose to completely adapt to the lifestyle of her husband's culture.

I began questioning my marriage and my future as I heard Michelle talk about her own disappointments and disillusions in her choices. Michelle was in her late thirties, approaching her forties and feeling stuck. I was afraid to fast forward to my forties and find that I was still in Saudi Arabia, married to Ahmed with three kids of my own, and no sense of purpose beyond controlled motherhood. I wondered how my friends—modern foreign women— felt about their lives with a Saudi husband. Were they stuck? Kim had a liberal and westernized husband and continued to live as an American woman unapologetically. Michi by contrast became more and more conservative and our way of viewing the world was drastically bifurcating. I felt stuck. I didn't think Michelle felt as stuck as I did. She always had the fallback of her country of birth. I didn't have that; I had to find it. It was comforting to have a friend with whom I could safely talk about such fears and worries, without the concern of being dismissed, judged, or betrayed.

I took a year off after leaving the school to contemplate my next career move. During that time, I continued to rely on Michelle's advice and friendship, and followed her suggestion to take on tutoring. Sarah, my only private pupil, was a nine-year-old girl with a German mother, and Saudi father. Her parents knew my parents, and after the Gulf War of '91, she lived in Germany with her mother and sisters for several years before returning to Saudi Arabia and enrolling in school, where she struggled with the Arabic language. So, I went from being an English teacher to tutoring Arabic.

Sarah came to my apartment several times a week after school. We spent a couple of hours each time working on her assignments and conversational skills. Fluent in German and English, Sarah was a very bright girl who struggled to adjust to her Saudi life. During the first few months of our time together, I strove to connect with her. She was negative, passive-aggressive, and unappreciative. When I once made the mistake of relevantly referring to Hitler in our history lesson, she went from her usual mute mode to lecturing me—initially in German, which I couldn't understand—about Hitler and the blasphemous act of mentioning his name. Message received, do not mention Hitler.

Each time I expressed kindness, she retaliated with snarky and defensive comebacks. For the first time, I found myself challenged in my ability to communicate with a child. I tried everything. Even my stern and hard-nosed approach did not work well with her. Eventually, I won her over with patience and compassion. When she saw that I empathized with her defensive reaction, she softened and felt heard. I ultimately established a way to communicate with her that fostered a peaceful outcome instead of conflict and resistance, a skill I revived with my teenage sons decades later.

Once again, I found myself in the learner's seat while claiming the title of teacher. Sarah grew increasingly more comfortable with her Arabic abilities as well as letting down her protective shield of aversion. She became so relaxed in my home that my dog Valentino, who normally hid in the kitchen when she arrived, would now sit in her lap while we did homework.

I strengthened my own competence in rational communication through this experience, especially with children who—like me—were clearly suffering from a sense of not belonging. Sarah reflected me, perhaps a savvier version of myself because she lived and experienced a full childhood in the West, and now found her wings clipped and her boundaries firm. I chose to embrace her as if she were a young me and offered all the reassurance I would have wanted for my young self.

My year as a tutor went by fast. I enjoyed the isolation but was ready to return to the workforce amongst adult peers. I was no longer interested in the school environment, and out of the three possible careers available to me—teacher, banker, and doctor—posing as a banker seemed doable with my limited education and experience. After an interview, I was offered the position of Personal Assistant to the General Manager of Operations—an all-women's department. There were eighty female employees on our floor, and we were segregated from the rest of the male colleagues at the bank. Ahmed worked in the Treasury Department of the bank, and both he and I were given grief from our coworkers because of my position as communicator between the women's and men's departments.

In my role as personal assistant, my daily duties included interacting with the personal assistant of the General Manager on the men's side, Jovi, who was from the Philippines. He was brilliant, funny, and extremely hard-working. He and I developed a great friendship, and he trained me when it was time to implement the email system and inter-bank web. At that time, I had not yet experienced the internet, and my early exposure to the idea of electronic mail and websites was in the exclusive system of the bank. Jovi and I emailed every day, several times a day, as we had the responsibility of facilitating communication between our bosses.

He was the first to send me a smiley face using punctuation marks :-) before it was an emoji, and he introduced me to many shortcuts and tricks of the trade when putting together a spreadsheet, a report, a memo, or a meeting proposal.

When, on rare occasions, one of the men came to the women's department for a meeting with a group of women or with our manager, all the women in our department covered up with their abayas. Many covered their faces too, but a few only covered their bodies and hair with abaya and hijab. I was the only female who did not cover. I chose not to wear the abaya or hijab and was usually the one who interacted the most with our male colleagues.

On one hand my behavior was daring and controversial; I knew that the majority of the women I worked with judged my decision not to cover. On the other hand, the men I interacted with were often Westerners, who missed no opportunity to tell me how much they appreciated being able to communicate with me and how at ease they felt knowing I was their go-to person in the Operations Department. It wasn't the case with all the men in the bank; I quickly realized that my Saudi colleagues were uncomfortable with my casual and non-conforming appearance. So out of respect, I decided to place a symbolic scarf on my head when I had to work with them. It was enough for these men to feel appeased, and for me to feel professional.

One morning there was great commotion in the office. I didn't know what was going on. I inquired, and one of the young women in the printing office told me, "The bank's CEO's niece was hired as the new Vice Manager, and she starts today! Did you know she is also married to her cousin, which makes the CEO her uncle and father-in-law?!"

No, I didn't know that, and I didn't care.

There was anticipation by all. The women wondered what this new boss would be like, and they hinted at how they could *suck up to her* and rub elbows with her. They seemed to have no filters for their feelings and desires of befriending this VIP who was about to arrive.

When this mighty, powerful woman finally entered the main operations room, you would think that the Marchioness of Hexham had arrived by the sight of all eighty plus women in the department lined up—like the downstairs servants in Downton Abbey—to meet her and be noticed. Before she began with the greetings, the six-foot tall, stunningly gorgeous young woman rushed to me, grabbed me affectionately, and hugged me tightly, exclaiming, "Jasmin, I had no idea you were working here! I'm so excited to see you!" she said, genuinely, and she meant it.

"Oh my god! Laila! I had no idea you were the big shot we've been waiting for all morning!" I said honestly while I laughed.

The women were struggling to lift their jaws off the ground. They were shocked and desperate to get Laila's attention. Laila introduced herself and shook hands with every single one of the women there. When she walked out of the room with the General Manager, all the women looked at me, and one of them, on behalf of all the others, exclaimed "What? You know her?"

"We went to school together and we've been in the same class since first grade," I said matter-of-factly.

It's true, Laila and I had known each other since first grade and had graduated high school together. She was also one of my mom's students. I knew she came from a wealthy family, but then, most of the girls I went to school with were either royal, noble, or wealthy. I was not fazed by her status, and it almost seemed ridiculous to me that all these women were star-struck by my life-long classmate. After that day I was viewed either as the coolest chick in the office, or the boss's pet. Neither label affected me since I had an established relationship with Laila. We worked closely together and shared an office.

Four weeks after my friend arrived, she replaced our manager, who was fired. Being privy to this information before it went into effect, I knew that the bank's administration was not content with our manager's performance, and I knew that Laila—a college graduate in business and economics—had been brought in as an interim until they hired the permanent new manager. Uninterested in the position full time or long term, Laila had joined the bank as a favor to her uncle/father-in-law.

A new mother, Laila was more focused on her growing family than on professional advancement. She enjoyed traveling and taking on project-based opportunities for the fun of it, certainly not for the money. I admired her tremendously. Laila was educated, modern, smart, kind, stylish, modest, humble, and stunningly beautiful. She was a true progressive Saudi woman. I couldn't be revered like her because I lacked the social status and resources that contributed to her influence, and because of that, my social and intellectual aspirations would not be acknowledged.

Laila and I had a history, and we became good friends after working together. I felt admired and appreciated by her. She felt safe and authentic with me. She knew I was not desperate for her attention like most of the women in the office, and she especially respected the fact that I never told her what I thought she wanted to hear. When work was slow and we had time on our hands, we would close the office door and chat.

Laila would open up about her marriage struggles, "It's hard to always say what I need and what I think, because when you're married to your cousin, his family is also your family, and it becomes so complicated."

I didn't say much about my struggles with Ahmed, but I hinted at my concerns about his family and the mounting pressure of having a child, despite my unreadiness. We also shared similar struggles with our fathers and their withdrawn personalities. It became clear how our childhoods affected our womanhood. One day she surprised me during one of our conversations, when she paused, looked at me in a gentle and loving way, and said, "I think you were born in the wrong country. You don't belong here. You really have to find a way out!"

I was shocked and unsure of what I said or did to prompt her to think that. But she'd known me since first grade. She knew my mother. Her observation was accurate, but it caught me off guard as we didn't know each other intimately. I was happy to hear those words. I felt validated and accepted by someone, who to a large extent, represented the society. No one had ever said anything like that before. To my surprise, she approved of who I was. This was not a common thing in my life and was perhaps another message from the universe that the clock was ticking. I had to seriously ponder the direction of my life with more confidence and, certainly, more courage.

PART THREE:

THE ATTAINMENT

THE UNTHINKABLE

By now, I knew this marriage was reaching the finish line. It was fast and exciting, but we'd taken all the laps we could, and I was ready to face that. Ahmed was not surprised when I admitted, "I think we must reevaluate some things. I don't think we share the same goals for our future anymore." The heat of an intense argument one evening moved me to be honest.

"You might be right. I don't think I am ready to give up though. I still think we should try everything we can to see if there is hope. Maybe we should see a therapist?" he asked sincerely.

"Okay. I am willing to give it a try. If anything, guidance on how to move forward would be good," I said cooperatively, feeling almost decided on the outcome.

I knew we would most likely not be working on repairing what was a natural drifting and parting of two people who were finally growing up and maturing into themselves. Ahmed found the phone number of an American therapist who worked at the American Community Services (ACS) in the diplomatic quarters in Riyadh.

At the ACS, where Ahmed and I attended social functions, we met Darryl, who rented office space for his private practice as a licensed psychotherapist. Ahmed and I were in crisis. After my mother-in-law suffered a scary medical event, Ahmed felt more attached to his family, and any plans he and I had to leave the country were fading, creating a stronger sense of urgency for me to move on.

When I walked into Darryl's office for the first time, we shook hands,

"Hi, I'm Darryl Faulk."

"I'm Jasmin" I replied—a mundane greeting, but the encounter was electrifying. I remember everything about the way he looked and smelled. The Hugo Boss cologne was exquisite and subtle. I immediately noticed his twinkling blue eyes and silky sandy hair that flowed to the top of his shoulders. I noticed his navy-blue suit and tie, with a dual flag pin of Saudi Arabia and The USA on the collar of his blazer. His charming groomed brown beard was enhanced by the gray highlights. When he smiled, I noticed his perfect teeth, which I found immensely attractive.

Seconds after our brief introduction, I remember hearing a sighing voice in my head, *"There you are!"* It was as if I had been looking for someone my whole life and had just now found him. There was an immediate familiarity, but even more profound than that, an unfamiliar allure. It took me several minutes to compose my mental state and refocus on the purpose of our encounter.

During that brief session Ahmed declared that I needed guidance in re-evaluating my priorities. I affirmed that our goals were no longer in alignment as a couple. My commitment was challenged by my continued dejection.

Darryl listened and gave no advice. He simply said that his role was to help facilitate a path along which Ahmed and I would journey. He assured us that, based on the work that we will do in counseling, we will either reach a point in which we walk together or go our separate ways. I liked that. Ahmed not so much.

After leaving Darryl's office that night, I could not stop thinking about him and felt embarrassed by my schoolgirl crush, which was all the more vivid and ironic as I felt crushed by the reminder of the painfully unfair life I lived as a woman with desires, hopes and dreams that, by design, were never going to be a reality. My reaction when meeting Darryl affirmed any and all doubts I had about my future with Ahmed. I became aware that the last thread attached to the marriage I was eager to end, was now coming undone. We attended just a couple of sessions before Ahmed decided it was not worth our time. His decision affirmed to me that our marriage was not worth our time—a thought I kept to myself while I assessed my options.

In the year after this brief encounter with Darryl, Ahmed and I remained married but grew farther and farther apart. We maintained a formal social life, and traveled, but avoided the pending question about our fate.

I wondered if he thought about our future like I did. I was no longer invested in our marriage and began to contemplate scenarios in my mind, both realistic and unrealistic.

I saw Darryl on occasion at the ACS, where I would go for events, movie nights, and shopping, and each time I saw him, I felt butterflies in my stomach and the odd sensation of hyperventilating crept up. I was confused but also enchanted by his gentle smile and charming interest in our brief and superficial conversations. I didn't think that thoughts were harmful, and I allowed myself to daydream of the unthinkable.

What if I could be with him? What if he felt the same? I would leave Ahmed in a heartbeat and move on with my life!

I didn't understand how such thoughts could have made their way into my psyche, when I knew nothing about Darryl, except that nothing about him was attainable. He was married, I was married. He was twenty-two years my senior. I was raised Muslim with the understanding that it would be a sin to marry a non-Muslim. But above all obstacles, he was American. This political glitch seemed to be the one hint of reality that kept me grounded when I floated into a fantasy land where I held Darryl's hand and ran my fingers through his hair and beard and planned a life of eternal bliss in a world that was never meant to be mine.

Before leaving the ACS one night, where Ahmed and I had attended a movie, he stopped to use the restroom while I sat in the car and waited. It was dark and quiet. I laid my head back on the seat's headrest and closed my eyes. I was startled by a sound that came from the car's front hood. I opened my eyes and saw that Darryl had walked by—heading home after a long day at work—and rolled his fingers on the hood of our car to get my attention. When our eyes met, he smiled, and that moment froze like a scene in a movie. I stopped breathing for a second and the sound of my heart beating was amplified in the silent vehicle. I knew in that moment that he too was struggling with feelings that we both recognized were forbidden and confusing.

With my thoughts often drifting to Darryl, and my marriage that stood no chance for revival, I decided to talk to Ahmed about divorce. I had reached the point where I knew I was not interested in just a separation. I knew this relationship had run its course. I knew that what fun we once had was part of our youthful naiveté and our own desperate desire to live a normal life in an environment that to us was abnormally repressive. Time, as often it does, had changed us both so much. Instead of adapting, I was increasingly frustrated and impatient with the conservative and oppressive reality that surrounded me, while Ahmed was sinking deeply into the male dominant culture that welcomed him and strived to help him plant permanent roots with career goals and social connections.

After picking me up from work one afternoon, in the car, I told Ahmed we had to talk. It was an unusually gloomy day, with a sandstorm on the horizon. The sky was red, the wind was strong, and the atmosphere was filled with awkward tension between us.

We sat in our living room, now darkened by the storm. I began with the highly clichéd spiel: *It's me, I've changed a lot the past few years, I feel like we no longer want the same things, we've grown a lot and we both deserve to be happy.* To my surprise Ahmed did not resist my talk this time. There was nothing in my words that he could dispute. Ahmed had been a good husband. He had strived to be a better man than most of the ones around him. But I was unhappy, despite his attempts at making me happy. He was not perfect, at least not perfect for me. We were not in love, and even though I believed he would have carried on and built a family without great disappointments, I refused to repeat the cycle of so many women I knew, including my own mother, who chose to sacrifice big parts of themselves for the families they so devotedly created. I wanted a family, but I didn't want the soul-sacrificing way to get it. I could no longer fake my way through society by willing myself into joy.

I was done.

As he listened quietly, I asked him to divorce me in accordance with the Islamic law of triple *talaq*, where a man tells his wife that he divorces her three times as a final and irreconcilable decision. Although we may not have been following all legal and official protocols in the privacy of our living room, we spontaneously followed what we had learned and heard about Islamic divorces from various religious schools of thought. This ritual was enough to affirm that it was happening before we took it to court. In that very moment, in the solitude of our home, the two of us committed verbally to end the marriage, a powerful symbol for me; it was my freedom from the marriage, a freedom I had to beg for. He had the power to impose the act with one word, while I had no such power without the orchestration of a legal battle.

I sat looking out the living room window at the sandstorm that had rolled in. The force of nature embodied in the sand wall made its way into our apartment, and my subconscious. I channeled the unstoppable strength with which the collective sand grains—now accumulating in my mouth— can plow through any and all obstacles. I was one with the grit of the sand. This was the very last time that I was to feel *less-than*. It was the conclusion of my long sentence of soul imprisonment, one which reminded me daily that my value was measured by inhumane and unfair standards. I wanted that moment to be the final time I would be humiliated and degraded in a society I never felt I belonged to. I had no idea what was in store for my future, but I knew without any hesitation that I was going to turn my life around at any cost and by any means. Like every sandstorm that eventually settles into moving dunes, I trusted that I would let my fate carry me where I needed to go. The dunes don't have a road, they have the wind that carries them and guides them. If I were to move forward in my life, I had to find my guiding wind.

Ahmed was cooperative, and he too recognized the inevitable change in ourselves. He expressed some sadness, and his pain was visible when any conversation about how to proceed took place. He decided immediately to explore the possibility of further studies in New York, perhaps as a test to see if I would reconsider staying in the marriage if he now promised to leave the country—a promise that he had first made almost nine years ago. He knew, however, that leaving the country was not going to save our marriage. While he displayed genuine signs of grief, I felt relief, and even some guilt, because I was not sad or regretful about the end of our young, albeit almost decade-long, relationship. We never stood a chance. Our union was based on cultural rules and religious boundaries, where couples who wanted to experience the meaning of romantic companionship and partnership—in a world that forbade it in every way outside of marriage—had to forfeit the natural instruction of primal courtship.

That night I went to bed feeling like a new person. No event in my life had made me feel more empowered and freer. I had become one of those women on the Oprah Winfrey Show. I heard Oprah's voice ring in my ears, her unshaken tone and powerful proclamation that every woman deserves to be free, to be happy, and to be the master of her destiny. I deserved to be free, to be happy, and to be the master of my own destiny. This was my opportunity, after years of secretly watching the show and planting seeds of Oprah's wisdom in my mind, which was no longer wasted entertainment, or worse yet, cruel torture. This was my time. The notion that "I've got nothing to lose" exploded forcefully in my core and rose above the fact that I was divorced, neither a mother nor a wife, and considered damaged goods. What I did have was the opportunity to claim my freedom and drastically change my life. For the first time I dreamed of the unthinkable. Devised the unimaginable.

I began plotting my escape from my country.

FRIDAY EMAILS

One evening during a break in my Hapkido class at the ACS, I ran into Darryl in the hall. He told me about his recent trip to Italy, where Rome seemed to have left a magical impression on him. I agreed, Rome is my favorite city in the world, anciently powerful and modernly stunning.

Darryl talked about the highlights of his trip, "It was incredible to see all the ancient buildings around me while I sat and enjoyed a glass of Italian wine." He was filled with awe.

"Yes! It's quite a sight, isn't it? What did you think about the Spanish Steps?" I said as I pictured him there enjoying the view at night with that glass of wine, or at the Trevi fountain tossing a make-a-wish coin.

His trip sounded wonderful, and he spoke with the enthusiasm of a true traveler. I wanted nothing more than to sit with him and talk more about travel, about Italy, even about the divine mysteries of life.

Before getting too lost in my head with that vision, I snapped out of it and proposed continuing the conversation next time I was going to be at the ACS, as I had to run back to my Hapkido class. In that brief conversation we also exchanged email addresses and, that same night when I went home, I found an email message in my Yahoo inbox. It was short and sweet:

> *Jasmin,*
> *I just want you to know that I think you are a very special person,*
> *and I am sure you are going to succeed at anything you set your*
> *mind to.*
> *Darryl*

I sat at the computer staring at his email as if it were a picture of his face. I was blushing and felt enraptured. I was excited he emailed so soon, and I wrote many drafts before finally replying.

Darryl,
Thank you for this kind message. It is well timed. I needed the encouragement as I move forward with my life. Ahmed and I have finally separated and the future is exciting and overwhelming!
I look forward to continuing our conversation about Italy!
Jasmin

From those two emails, the "Friday emails" were born.

During those days I spent my evenings and weekends surfing the *world wide web*, which had only been recently launched in Saudi Arabia. The internet was aggressively censored, and any hint of political or sexual content was immediately blocked. This left room for unexpected curiosities. I found myself in chatrooms, one in particular, that was dedicated to Michael Jackson fans. I joined the group anonymously, using the name "Tabloid Hater" in reference to a Michael Jackson song, "Tabloid Junkie."

I spent months in that chatroom meeting MJ fans from all over the world, we talked about many things, mainly King of Pop trivia, fun facts, and speculated about the possibility that Michael was also in the chatroom under a secret identity. It was not MJ all the time though; some of the members found a comforting community in the chatroom, and often shared their struggles with bullies and difficult family relationships. I was too conditioned by my environment to disclose anything personal about who I was, where I lived, and what my intimate ambitions were. In fact, I was so ambiguous that many wondered and asked about my gender, my age, and my nationality. I always answered with playful enigmatic riddles. They never learned anything about my true identity. This made me one of the most popular members of the chatroom group. I had become known as "Tabsy" and before too long, I was one of the top cronies who many other members confided in.

I enjoyed being mysterious and androgynous. There was a degree of innocent public flirting between many of the group's members, and I thrived in the ambiguity of my persona which made flirting with both boys and girls in that safe group a great way to fine tune my future skills as a flirt with life. I realized that flirting and playing was not only meant for sexual arousal or intimacy, but quite the contrary, it became a way to affectionately relate to others with zest and purity. Over the years I mastered the art of platonic flirting which, as a half-Italian, was part of my genetic make-up. I attribute that quality of beguilement and banter to many of my meaningful friendships with women, men, children and even animals.

Darryl and I happened to be online at the same time the day after our brief email exchanges. It was a Friday—the weekend in Saudi Arabia—and during our internet surfing, we started emailing back and forth in real time. I was quickly less active in the MJ chatroom and enchanted by his attention making its way into my Yahoo.

Ahmed and I were still sharing the apartment and our plans to separate had not yet been announced to our families. He was spending the whole day with his family, and I chose to have a "me day" at home. Darryl's wife was at work for a twelve-hour shift.

The emails were fun, inspiring, intellectually stimulating, playful, and a little flirtatious. Most of all, they were a huge trigger to my personal awakening. I felt deep joy. I was smitten, and so was he. Even though I kept strict boundaries and safe measures, I had never experienced this kind of romantic sensation, like fireworks going off each time a new email from his Hotmail account showed up in my inbox. We spent a solid ten hours at the computer that day. Not including an hour when I made myself some food and he ran to the store to buy a new keyboard because his two-year-old son had accidentally knocked over the tea mug and fried the one he was using. I enjoyed messaging with him because I was attracted to him, but also because it was refreshing to be able to talk to a man and know what it's like to interact with someone of the opposite sex without all the cultural rules and restrictions that had always stood in my way.

The last email he sent me that night was a cryptic FYI, in which he clarified why he felt comfortable having this exchange with me all day despite being a married man. He said his marriage was "actually over, I live with Vicky, my wife, in an amicable separation for the sake of our son." I didn't feel like I had disrespected or violated their marriage because we chatted like new friends that felt so familiar, but I did sigh a sigh of relief at his statement.

Later he explained that they were not announcing their separation because it would jeopardize their housing accommodations—as expats in Saudi—where they were able to jointly live in one house with their young son; if they were officially divorced or separated, Vicky would have to be in single women's housing, and it would make things very hard for little Zachary. While I was glad to hear this, it didn't really matter much. Our emails did not violate any rules of conduct. They were amicable and fun, and in no way inappropriate.

That said, it was clear that both of us longed to explore our feelings for each other. I was nervous about having my heart broken over a future that might never be. And he, as he confessed later, kept his distance for fear that I was a decoy from the Saudi government to lure him and then have him arrested and punished. The list of "don'ts" that Westerners are handed, before arriving in Saudi Arabia for work, is a long one, but the one thing that stood out to him the most from that list was: "Don't ever pursue a Saudi woman, in friendship or romance! It is a punishable crime!"

We were now both put to a harsh test. I kept thinking *life is too short! I am not going to overthink any of this.* He mirrored my recklessness and decided that the risk outweighed his fear, and not so long after the Friday emails, he asked if we could talk on the phone.

"I don't want to go to my grave and not know what it feels like to kiss you," was his opening line during our first phone conversation after weeks of romantic emails.

"I, I … I feel the same," I replied, mortified.

That week I went to the ACS with my parents' driver, to pick up an item that I had ordered from one of the local artists, and, of course, not knowing if he was there, had hoped to see Darryl. The "do not disturb" sign that he used when seeing a client was not displayed. I knocked on his office door, and when he opened it, he smiled wide, not expecting to see me there.

His office was a comforting place, dimly lit and scented with Nag Champa incense. There was a desk, blue furniture: two armchairs, and a love-seat. Beautiful art as well as his various diplomas decorated the white walls. Plants of all sizes also brought a sense of eco-therapy in his sacred space.

He invited me in, and I hesitantly said, "Okay, just for a few minutes, I really need to go, my driver has been waiting outside for a while."

We sat for a few minutes not saying a word, looking into each other's eyes from across the room and breathing in meditative contemplation. He stood up and walked out of the office to get a bottle of water from the kitchen, saying he would be right back. It had been over a year since I was in his office as a short-lived client with my now soon-to-be-ex-husband. Many things had changed. I was shaking. I couldn't believe I was in his office, alone and without a therapeutic purpose.

When Darryl came back, he sat in the armchair to my right, a change from the one on the left where he usually sat, in the role of therapist. I was on the loveseat. He was visibly nervous too, and the sounds of our hearts beating echoed in the quiet room. We looked into each other's eyes for a few more minutes, when he finally said, "All the stars in the universe have aligned so perfectly, just so we could meet and find ourselves right here, right now." He paused, then continued, "This was written in the stars," a reference to an Elton John song, his favorite artist.

I couldn't find words to respond to his poetic charm and signaled with my hand for him to come sit next to me. When he did, I could no longer look into his dreamy blue eyes. I felt vulnerable and astonished that I was willingly breaking the boundary that had stood between us for over a year. He gently put his hand on my shoulder, and, without any warning, I impulsively and helplessly fell into his embrace. On my way into his arms, our lips united like long-lost lovers. I had kissed only two other men before Darryl, but I had never experienced it like I did in that moment. Everything froze in time. Our embrace was so powerful it almost scared us. He gasped for air at one point—the overwhelmingly intense encounter triggered his asthma for a few seconds. I knew that very moment that we were falling desperately in love. Falling because we could no longer stand still on the edge of that cliff of yearning. Desperate, because neither of us knew what that meant or what would ever come out of it.

THE BOY FROM ALABAMA

By now, Ahmed and I were no longer relating like husband and wife. Not long after our decision, he left for New York where he stayed with his best friend, Rashon, and explored what options a life in New York offered him. I was staying in our apartment by myself, going to work daily, and talking to Darryl on the phone in the evenings. Our time together evolved into occasional visits, where I would secretly sneak him into my apartment or visit him at his office. It was exciting and scary, but I was resigned to the notion that if my life were in danger, it was worth it.

Darryl and I started to relate like lovers and talk like best friends. In the first few weeks of our courtship, we let down our veils and opened up about our life stories, painting a picture of who we were and who the characters in our lives were. I wasn't sure what the future held, but I was sure of one thing, I didn't want to miss out on any moment shared with him. Our phone calls lasted hours. We talked about everything.

"I was born in Monroeville Alabama, where Harper Lee lived," he shared. "Growing up in the deep south was tough. I was a military brat; my daddy was a pilot in the air force and when I was six, we moved to Okinawa in Japan."

"Why don't you have a southern accent though?!" I asked as I giggled.

"I did when I was younger, my mom still does, my whole family does, but I wanted to move away from it all. I headed west after high school. I surfed for a year in California, and then settled in Nevada a few years where I was a youth minister in a church," he continued.

"A youth minister?!" I said, surprised.

"I wanted to please my mom; she is very religious. I actually led vinyl breaking sessions during that time! I missed out on being a total hippie because I was too busy judging it all. My loss!" he laughed.

I was intrigued. He had lived multiple lives, and now he was here in Saudi Arabia! I wanted to know everything about him, as I cautiously shared about myself and my limited life experiences.

His father, Willi Dempsey, "Expressed no interest or ability in being a father; he barely knew me. He was either deployed or drunk," Darryl started off before bursting into laughter and continuing with, "He once took me on a Cessna when I was a teenager. He piloted that damn thing while chugging on a bottle of whiskey he kept tucked by his side."

But this inadequacy as a father conceivably came from the lack of role models in Dempsey's youth, since losing his own father at the age of two. Darryl never knew his paternal granddaddy, and grew up fearing his maternal granddaddy Ike, who was 6' 7" tall and imposed intimidation beyond his height.

Darryl playfully broke into a southern accent when telling these stories, imitating his mother Vernell, "She would say: don't you cry like a little girl now! Boys don't cry like that!" Like me, he grew up feeling isolated and alone, but his coping mechanisms were self-destructive; by his own account, he learned to lie his way out of all situations since toddlerhood because it was "the only way to avoid a beating with a belt."

I was shocked when Darryl casually told me that in 1978 his mom, and her second husband Bill, lived in Riyadh just a few miles from my childhood home. Bill was in the military, and they were stationed there for a couple of years. I was four years old at the time, clueless about the mysteries that life would send my way. I enjoyed listening to Darryl's stories. His voice, sweet and calm, and his chuckle sincere and warm. I had never met a man who had an ease about him like Darryl did. *Was this a trait in American men?* I wondered. Getting to know him was eye-opening in so many ways, in particular as a woman learning how to be engaged with a world beyond the limited and enclosed one I had grown up in.

One of the ways that we shared our love for one another was through cards and mix-cassette tapes. Of the songs I shared with him, he especially loved Emma Shapplin's operatic "Spente Le Stelle." He played me a song by Sarah McLachlan the first time we spoke on the phone, a song that he said made him think of me since the day we met.

Every moment marked with apparitions of your soul
I'm ever swiftly moving tryin' to escape this desire
The yearning to be near you, I do what I have to do
But I have the sense to recognize that I don't know how to let you go
I don't know how to let you go
A glowing ember burning hot and burning slow
Deep within I'm shaken by the violence of existing for only you
I know I can't be with you, I do what I have to do

Our phone calls became a sanctum. Our intimacy grew through this medium. But we craved each other's company and longed for a physical connection. I was afraid of exploring sexual pleasure with him because the idea of being with a man I was not married to terrified me. Darryl was understanding and said there was no pressure. I wanted to feel ready, which in my mind was never going to be while we were still in the Kingdom. We decided to spend a whole weekend together just to experience the pleasures of sharing a meal, watching a movie, and snuggling. I snuck Darryl into my apartment after he picked up food at one of his favorite Indian restaurants. After dinner I made popcorn, and we watched *Titanic* while cuddling. It felt so natural to be with him. I was happy and safe in his presence. The world did not exist outside of our little bubble.

In these moments, time stood still. In the back of my mind, I knew I could not throw my life away because I was falling in love with a man I didn't know how I could ever be with. I struggled to balance myself between the temptation that he represented and the freedom I hungered for. From the moment Ahmed and I agreed to separate, I began developing scenarios for myself in which I could orchestrate a successful escape. I didn't have the heart to tell Darryl that I was doing so, because I didn't know what "we" were; what was happening between us was not part of the plan. But I knew that in this very moment I didn't want to think about anything else. The harsh reminder of the extreme urgency since childhood to pursue freedom resurfaced as I lay in bed alone at night, with Valentino now by my side. I agonized over the cruelty of my predicament.

THE VANISHING ACT

Having nothing to lose and falling in love became the two powerful ingredients to formulate the ultimate illusion: my vanishing act.

As the weeks progressed, Darryl and I started talking about a future together, as inconceivable as it was. Although we were rushing into it, we were propelled by a frightening taboo that had forced us to live with pent-up feelings that emphasized our desire to pursue personal and joint happiness. After my separation from Ahmed, I started plotting my secret escape, and of the many scenarios I entertained, I wanted to go with the one that didn't openly put my life in danger. Therefore, I had my spyglass pointing towards Canada, where my lifelong friend, Cybèle, had been living since leaving Saudi Arabia. Cybèle offered me a place to stay upon my pending arrival in Canada, where I was hoping to find a job and fully immigrate. My parents knew that I hoped to visit Cybèle, and that was enough to grant me the necessary documentation to travel without raising suspicion.

I envisioned myself living in a city, where the winters are brutal and jarringly opposite of what I had always known. The idea of a long snowy season and dark days may not have been my first choice but being covered in a parka to stay warm in the snow seemed far more appealing than being covered in an abaya in the heat of the Arabian desert for the rest of my life. I pictured myself removed from my privileged surroundings, taking odd jobs to make ends meet and embracing the struggles of the immigrant who, above all, seeks freedom despite losing all the foundational comforts of family, home, and familiarity.

Cybèle and I spoke in codes, both on the phone and in letters. We were young and far less concerned with a second plan if things didn't work out. There was no possibility for failure, and the plan was to succeed regardless of what it required. Cybèle's attitude was: *Sure! Come on over, we'll figure it out!* And that's just what I needed at that time. My attitude was: *I don't care what it takes, I have to get out of here!* And that's what kept me focused and determined. In reality, there was no plan. I was to pack up, convince my father I wanted to go visit Cybèle in Canada, and never come back. Once I got to Canada, the real planning would begin.

No one—except for Cybèle and Darryl—knew of my Canadian scheme. As Darryl and I became more affixed to one another, he decided to end his contract in Riyadh and return to the United States sooner than planned with the hope that it would keep us closer. I told him I was leaving for Canada by mid-summer, and we negotiated ways to maintain a long-distance relationship until things seemed stable enough for one of us to relocate.

He began searching for jobs online somewhere in the Western part of the United States, because he loved the years he spent in Colorado.

"What do you think of Wyoming?" He asked.

"Cowboys? Horses? Sounds exciting!" My imagination traveled to the old Disney documentaries and John Wayne westerns I watched longingly as a child.

"I have a phone interview with a community college for a position as a psych nurse professor, and if it goes well, I think we can plan a new life together in Wyoming, I've never lived there. It will be *our* thing," he said, with hope.

I was not preoccupied with the location so much, Canada or Wyoming, it was all North America; it was all symbolic of freedom, of trees, no abaya, and a happily-ever-after castle-in-the-sky. I had only seen the Eastern part of the country, and what little visual I had of the rest came from movies and books. At this point, Wyoming started to sound a lot like Canada with its long snowy winters, but also, ironically, a lot like Saudi Arabia, with its arid hot summer deserts.

Darryl tried hard to be supportive and respectful of my plans, but his decision to sacrifice his security and compromise his time with his young son to be closer to me, made me seriously evaluate his proposal of joining him in Wyoming from the start, and setting aside Canada. I reconsidered my plans and wondered about the temptation of trusting him and the choices he was making for both of us. I was nervous about, once again, depending on a man for my ultimate freedom, but I also felt pressured by the insanity of romantic infatuation. I resisted the thought of the staggering responsibility that came with being a stepmother. Darryl reassured me it would all work out with little Zachary and with Vicky, who was planning to remain in Saudi Arabia for at least a few more years. Zachary would spend half the year with us, and the other half with Vicky. Was I ready to parent a child who was so young and potentially confused about all the changes in his life? I had no time to think about the answer.

Going to Canada was a straightforward plan. It didn't include exes and children. It depended on me and my ability to make it work. I was going to ask my father for permission to visit Cybèle in Canada, and he would oblige by writing the letter of permission, which was required for every woman planning to travel alone outside of the country. With my plans now taking on a new direction, I had to think fast and hard for a solid, foolproof device to accomplish this arrangement. It all boiled down to trusting the unknown, but most of all, trusting myself.

Western Wyoming Community College had offered Darryl a job during the phone interview, but I was not having as smooth a time as Darryl was with marking things off my checklist. Ahmed, who was still in New York, was not cooperating. He called me from New York, where he had originally planned to stay for three months and asked me to reconsider and give our marriage a second chance, a proposal that caught me off guard and totally blindsided me. Alarmed by his persistence, I firmly declined his offer, and he became angry. I still lived in our apartment, expecting to have some time on my own before we divorced. But that night, those plans took a sharp turn.

In a rage, Ahmed said, "If you don't want to stay married, then I advise you to pack up and get out of *my* house. I am getting on the next plane to Riyadh, and if you are still there, it's not going to be good!"

I called my mom in hysterics and asked her to send over the driver and maid to help me pack. It was 10 pm. I struggled to sort through my personal belongings and the sentimental items I had collected over our six-year marriage. On one hand, I was glad I didn't have much time to be emotional, but on the other hand, the frenetic rush caused me to feel detached from everything I owned, and a sense of emptiness took over. I never went back to the apartment after that night; what I managed to take with me were my personal lifelong treasures only. I left our joint acquisitions behind, including our wedding album, souvenirs of our global travels, and the CD collection we both loved so much.

I returned to my parents' home that night. It was also the night before Darryl was heading to the airport to fly back to the U.S. and visit the college. The only comforts I had in that moment were the notion that Darryl was making plans for our soon-to-be life together and my mother's dependable support, paired with Valentino's cuddles. It felt safe to be home. This was the home I'd known since birth, the place where the greatest joys and deepest sorrows took place. Despite the challenges and dysfunctions of our family dynamics, I always felt unquestionable security in my parents' presence. We shared an instinctive love as family members. We accepted our flaws and dismissed our shortcomings. I didn't want to live there forever—in fact, I was so eager to leave that I married at nineteen—but I knew that with time our family always succeeded in healing wounds and accepting fate as it unfolded.

The next evening, I sat in my mother's living room with Valentino in my lap, still agitated from the surreal unravelling of the last twenty-four hours after Ahmed's call. I heard a faint whistle, Valentino jumped off my lap and ran out of the door. It was Ahmed, who made good on his promise to catch the next flight and had the balls to show up at my parents' home, unannounced. He walked in the living room, and quickly reassured my visibly flustered mother that he came in peace. Reluctantly, my mom left the room so that he and I could talk.

Ahmed sat across from me and began by apologizing for his behavior on the phone the night before. I refused to look at him and said nothing. He continued by saying that poor judgment came over him and grief clouded his thoughts; he realized the marriage was over and he was there to say goodbye to me and Valentino. He then chuckled and said, "And, you're not going to believe this. When I got off the plane, I had the biggest sign. I saw Darryl at the airport, do you remember Darryl?"

My heart stopped. *What does he mean? Oh my god! He saw Darryl, I wonder what Darryl is feeling?!!*

"Yeah, so?" I managed to cough out.

"Remember how we went to him over a year ago thinking about fixing our marriage? And he told us that we would meet a fork in the road? Seeing him is a sign!! A sign that we both have to move on, each of us taking their path at that fork! Don't you see that?!"

It was a bigger sign than that, actually.

Ahmed promised to cooperate and help me move on. I thanked him and expressed my appreciation. I also wanted the brief encounter to end swiftly and smoothly. He was there for about fifteen minutes. Saying goodbye to Valentino ended up being a harder task than saying goodbye to me. He shared his parents' disappointment in the outcome of our decision, and said, "My father is especially distraught, we had to rush him to the hospital with tightness in his chest."

In the last six hours Ahmed had arrived in Riyadh, crossed paths with Darryl at the airport, gone to his parents' home, given them the news, rushed his dad to the hospital, made sure his dad was ok, and come by my parents' home to say goodbye to me and Valentino. He did it all with a kind and calm attitude after the crazy phone call the night before. I could only imagine that during the fourteen-hour flight back from New York, he had time to think, and possibly sleep.

However, I didn't trust his attitude, and feared it was the calm before the real storm.

Just minutes after Ahmed left, Darryl called me from the airport in Jeddah where he had a brief layover. Sounding panicked, he said, "You'll never believe who I saw at the airport in Riyadh!"

"I know, it's ok, he just left my house, he's going to cooperate, don't worry," I said calmly.

"Are you sure he's not going to try to get you back? I'm going to be so far away, I am worried, sweetheart," he said, sounding vulnerable.

"You have nothing to worry about," I reiterated as we said goodbye before he boarded his second plane to New York.

Ahmed did not keep his promise. I learned a lot about human fragility during that time, from my own whirlwind of emotions, but also from observing Ahmed's struggle to relinquish a life imagined. Looking back, I recognize that we each dealt with grief in different ways. Life's experiences have a way of humbling us, and I have had my fair share of chagrin.

I was not able to see or understand Ahmed's pain at the time, and his behavior was disturbingly provoking as I sat desperately awaiting his cooperation, without which I could not legally or socially do anything to move on. I expected him to produce the legal divorce papers that same week, and with that, I also asked that he give me my passport—which as my legal guardian he possessed—as well as my financial assets that were tied to our joint account, exclusively under his name. I felt like I was running out of time as I scrambled to establish my legal guardianship, once again, under my father, who was more likely than my husband to agree to my request to travel. I was in limbo until my brother, Yasser, called Ahmed and, in a few words, gave him no option but to follow through with my expectations. Within days, I received my divorce paper, my passport, and my funds. Like he had done before, Yasser showed up for me and smoothed the path that I had been forced to walk upon, a gesture I always appreciated.

My brother was often a source of stress and resentment for me during my teens, but when he wore his hero's cape, I realized my rancor towards him was in essence toward the environment that I saw symbolized in him. The patience and respect Yasser and I displayed toward one another over the years fostered a powerful relationship, one that eventually erased all the mutual antagonism. Thanks to Yasser's imposition on Ahmed, I finally checked off some things from that list, making room in my head for the plan I had carefully devised. Once I received my divorce document—which is a legal letter from an Imam, stating Ahmed's desire to divorce me, with several male witnesses' signatures and no requirement from me other than to wait patiently for the piece of paper—Ahmed and I never spoke again.

That was the end. The end of my first *love* story, the end of my first long-term relationship, the end of a partnership that mutually served two young and lost identities in a world that never felt like theirs. The end of young trust and naïve expectations. The end of the life that was formulated so securely by my culture and family, and yet the end of the life I saw as a spiritual prison and social cave, where on occasion I had been allowed to go out and see daylight and hear birds sing. The end that signaled a mysterious and unimaginable beginning. I was going to leave the dark cave and stand on the edge of a cliff, throwing all caution to the wind and jumping into a freefall. There were no guarantees.

Ahmed became a stranger after nine years of being the center of my life. Later, I heard that he remarried, and with his new Saudi wife, happily started a family and career that took him places within Saudi Arabia and around the world. I was happy to know he accomplished his dreams, and not sure that he ever wondered what became of me.

Everything I had planned and weighed thus far sat on one side of a scale, and what I was about to do next, sat on the other side. I wished I didn't need to twist the truth and lie to my father, but I saw only one way out. I battled between my guilt and my survival. I trusted that my father loved me enough to one day forgive me. I knew my intentions to leave and start a new life mirrored the morals and ethics that my parents had instilled in me, all the while my actions contradicted their ideas of how I would accomplish that life. My father limited his hopes for me to seeing me fulfill his dreams within our cultural confines. My parents never realized, or maybe never admitted, that our bicultural experience was the gift—or perhaps the curse—that left me needing a worldlier ipseity.

The final stage of my planning required my shrewd skills and unapologetic spirit. I called upon the one person I trusted and knew would do anything for me, my cousin Vince in Italy.

Vince agreed to call my father and ask for his authorization to allow me to travel with him and his fiancé to the U.S. for a two-week—make-believe—vacation. This was the only way I knew I could get a visa to the U.S. with my father's consent.

My father hesitated but was willing to roll with it. He knew I had been to the States many times with Ahmed, making me an asset to Vince during this presumed trip; he also knew that I needed a vacation after the tumultuous weeks I had leading up to my divorce.

I was on pins and needles as my parents discussed the trip. The fact that I would be with my cousin, a trustworthy adult male, reassured my father. My father was a pleaser and loved people, but few had his absolute trust. Even though Vince was the precocious and playful toddler who couldn't keep the secret of my parents' courtship from our grandparents, he became the nephew my father respected and the cousin I could count on. In some ways, Vince and his Saudi uncle were alike: both quiet and pensive, both reserved and deeply caring, both limiting their conversations to the basic matter and condensed subject. I knew a dialogue between them about my travels would be brief and safe from too much questioning.

By now my mom knew of my actual plans; she knew I was suffering and prayed for my happiness and peace. She also trusted and encouraged me to proceed even as she concealed my intentions. I struggled with the position I had put her in. She was partially torn but drew strength from the rebel within her who had made bold choices back in her day and who now allowed me to have the same dignified opportunity after watching me genuinely try and fail to find joy in the culture she strived to make my own. I have her to thank for the courage and determination I inherited, but also for the unwavering support she has always offered her children.

Once I had the visa from the U.S. embassy—that my father thankfully never looked at closely because it was a six-month prospective student visa—and travel permission letter that my father wrote, I had a one-way ticket to my freedom. As I prepared for my trip, which would start at the Riyadh airport, I couldn't stop thinking about the fate of the Saudi Princess Mishaal bint Khaled Al Saud, who in 1977, at the age of 19 was caught at the airport and eventually executed for attempting to escape with a young commoner she had fallen in love with. While I was relieved that my father was clueless, I was distressed about the shrewdness of the Saudi government. My father was a big-hearted man; he was sensitively reserved, and I hoped I would convince him one day that my happiness was what he also wanted for me, despite his cultural and social concerns. I could not ask him for permission, but I imagined a day that I would be able to persuade him to forgive. Both of my parents had now approved my *mini vacation* to the U.S. I was to fly to Italy first and spend time with my relatives before leaving with Vince—*meeting Darryl in Milan*—and landing in New York, where I knew lady liberty would be waiting for me.

THE AIRPORT

I always dreaded airports. Since childhood all my trips to, from, and, through any airport were an augury of temporary freedom, and of my return to a dreaded reality. With my letter of permission and boarding pass in hand, passport ready, bags packed, and abaya on, I got into the car for what was to be my last drive to King Khaled International Airport in Riyadh to catch a red eye to Milan. I couldn't say farewell to anyone because this was meant to be a short trip. I had to suppress my agony over leaving Valentino, not knowing if I'd ever see him again.

My mom accompanied me as our family driver routinely drove us, unaware that it was our last goodbye. My mom tried to distract me, sensing my panic and fear about what might go wrong at the last minute. She talked about random things, and I could barely follow her. I hyperventilated internally and breathed deeply externally. I opened my backpack multiple times, confirming that I had all my papers, documents, and passport. Tucked in a hidden pocket were all my other personal documents: birth certificate with notarized translation, high school diploma with notarized translation, divorce paper with notarized translation, and professional resume with letters of recommendation and notarized translations. My life narrowed down to these pieces of paper that gave me a sense of authority, an awareness that felt overwhelmingly unfamiliar, given that my identity had always existed under the guardianship of my father or husband.

This was the pre-9/11 era. Going through security was less about terrorist threats and more about identity fraud. My mom was able to go through with me and walk all the way to the gate of my departure. As the traveler holding a boarding pass, I was taken to the *women's only* inspection room. There, officials asked that I uncover my face so they could confirm my identity and asked me to remove my abaya for a full pat-down. I disassociated, looking at the women agents most likely hired without any law-enforcement training. I observed them closely, knowing this would be my last time experiencing such a circumstance. They spit pumpkin seed shells on the floor and gossiped about other women while repeatedly mentioning Allah in immortal humility. This was an image that to the rest of the world—and soon to me—was so foreign, a reality from which I always felt severed.

My mom and I sat holding hands and smiling excitedly at one another, both hiding an understandable degree of sadness knowing that soon thousands of miles would come between us. As they called for boarding, I stood up, took a deep breath, and then sank back in panicked fear when I saw a large group of *Mutawa* strolling around the airport. Their signature short thobes, and long beards produced major anxiety for a lot of women and young men as they imposed their mandatory laws and carried out immediate consequences that often, involved violence and humiliation.

All I could think of in that moment was *they know my plans and they are here to arrest me,* as had happened to others in the past. I had never heard of a successful escape before me. The stories we heard were of women attempting to run away, only to be caught and punished, often executed. Was I the next statistic?

The thirty seconds between noticing them a few yards away from me and my mother's farewell embrace felt like an eternity. In a few seconds, my mother realized what had me paralyzed with terror. Without ever directing her glance at them, she pulled me close to hug me goodbye and whispered in my ear, "Just think, this will be the last time you see them! Go start a new life away from it all."

Fighting back tears and holding my breath, I took my seat on the SwissAir plane, intentionally having chosen a European airline, and started reciting my flight prayers as the plane sped down the runway. *Had I actually made it out safely?* The fear of being caught replaced my aviophobia, which I developed after the recent midair collision of Saudi Flight 763 with

Kazakistan Airlines flight 1907, which killed 349 passengers in the world's deadliest crash. I closed my eyes and clenched my fists. The force of the takeoff pushed me against my seat, and it was as if I was flying for the first time; but I was flying for the first time, *alone*. When we reached our desired altitude and the seatbelt signs went off, I loudly sighed and removed my abaya, knowing for sure I was safe. I stared out the window watching the beautiful desert of my birth-land, not knowing if I would ever set foot on it again. It was magnificently stunning, a part of the earth, like so many others, that was never meant to be distorted by human behavior and cultural practices.

ARRIVEDERCI

I landed in Milan.

When I saw my cousin Vince, and I could smell the signature aroma of Italian cities—a mixture of fuel, cigarettes, and espresso—I realized that I was finally surrounded by Italian people, my people, and I felt an abatement of worry. I knew it was real and that I had finally fled. I savored the surrealness of being there, a brief sensation that lasted until we arrived at my aunt's house, when reality hit.

Vince had seemed unusually reserved during our forty-five-minute drive from the airport in Milan to his parents' home in Brescia. He asked about my plans and expressed genuine support, but he was vague in his responses when I asked about his and the rest of the family's wellbeing.

When we arrived and I saw Zio Bertino, my aunt's husband and Vince's father—who always embraced me with genuine joy—I was taken aback by his distant and unfriendly greeting, as if he were not happy to host me for the week. Inside my aunt's house, her mother-in-law, Nonna Maria, welcomed me tearfully and whimpered in her edentulous southern dialect, "Go see your Zia, it will do her some good to see you."

Perplexed at the bizarre behavior by everyone I encountered, I hoped to feel at home once I saw my mother's sister. When I walked in the living-room, the sight of my aunt stupefied me. In one of the armchairs, facing the balcony that looked out on the garden, Zia Flora sat, frail, bald, and barely aware. No one else walked in the living-room with me. When my aunt asked,

"Who is it?" she struggled to see, having lost sight in one eye a few years earlier after an eye stroke.

I approached her and said, "It's me, Jasmin ... Zia."

"Oh, Jasmin, I am so happy you're finally here. I've been waiting for you! But I don't understand what all this nonsense of divorce and you leaving for America is about!"

Clearly Vince had updated his mother. Her comment did not sound like my gregarious aunt, but then, again, she did not look like herself, either.

I walked out of the room to go unpack, and when Vince saw the jolted look on my face, he said, "If you don't think you can stay here all week, just let me know, and I'll come pick you up. You can stay in Milano with me for a few days, not just the night before you leave."

What was going on? Was I missing something?

I soon called my mom to let her know that I had arrived. Horrified, I said to her in English—so that my Italian relatives could not overhear me—"Mamma! I think Zia Flora has cancer!!"

"Oh. You think so?" Was my mother's measured reply.

Everyone in the family had known about my aunt's year-long journey with brain cancer, but no one had told me. A couple of days later, when I confronted Vince, he admitted that the whole family believed I would have had the hardest time with the news and had agreed to shelter me from it. They also didn't anticipate my visit, and no one knew how to tell me before my arrival. This was one of the biggest blows of my life. I was stunned at the sight of my aunt, and the reality of her progressed illness. I was angry that no one had thought it right to inform me and prepare me for what I was about to see, because it turned out to be an even bigger shock than it would have been finding out about her illness in the first place. I later acknowledged that they were coming from a place of caring, knowing how traumatic Nebras' illness and death—from the very same condition my aunt now dealt with— had been for me.

Despite my deep desire to run away to Vince in Milan, I stayed with my Zia for the whole week. I helped wash her, change her, and every night, at her request, I read to her from my mom's self-help published books. I tied a scarf on her head and took her out on walks in her wheelchair around the block where I had spent so many childhood summers picking pinecones off the sidewalks and smelling them, running around with friends and sometimes crank-bell-ringing people's homes at night before running off shamelessly, petting random dogs on walks, riding bikes, and reading magazines on low concrete fence walls in the neighborhood. Not knowing when I would be back again, I savored each moment with my Zia, fearing it would be the last. When her friends came to visit her in the afternoon and commented on how happy she must be to have her favorite niece visiting, she would reply, "Yes, let's hope Jasmin's visit can perform a miracle."

I couldn't deliver on her hope for a miracle. As a child, I imagined my Zia was indomitable. Yet as I grew older, I realized that she was far less gutsy and determined than her younger sister, my mother. She was fragile in many ways and despite my grandfather's progressive influence, she was surprisingly old-fashioned and accommodating. To others, she gave so much of her big heart. From her, I inherited the comfort of talking to strangers on the street, on the bus, and in shops. My last days with her threw me into a melancholy reverie, as I recounted the many ways she enriched my life. Now heading towards a bold and unknown future, I savored the happy memories of my challenging childhood, of which she played a big and comforting part. We spent quiet hours in her garden where she convalesced by her hydrangeas and I relived our time together, recalling when I tagged along during her morning errands to pick up bread, fresh vegetables, deli meats or cheese, and listened to her give the store owner updates on my grandmother. I proudly grinned when she introduced her "oldest niece visiting from Saudi Arabia." She was affable and charming. She took care of vacation plans and family reservations when we all went to the beach, the lake, or the mountains. She taught me how to love the family farm, where she cultivated a little vineyard, a vegetable garden, and her chickens, which she released each Sunday morning when we visited, and called back to the coop before we left at sunset. Every summer as she and my Zio prepared for their grape harvest in the fall to make wine, she would ask me to squeeze my skinny body into the very large wine barrels in the cellar so I could clean them; often this meant picking up spindly spiders by the legs and carrying them out of the barrels alive so they wouldn't drown in grape juice in a few weeks' time. My Zia was a passionate beekeeper, and together we visited the hives where for the first time I wore a beekeeper's suit that protected me from getting stung, while my mom and May unfortunately, unprotected, had to bear the wrath of those protective bees. She made a zucchini frittata and custard-filled cake like no one else could. She loved her pond fish, Cleo—named after the fish in *Pinocchio*, her favorite book— which we always went to visit mid-day when everyone else was taking a nap at the farmhouse, and which she later confessed was, "A different fish each year because they can't really live too long in that small pond or survive the cold winters of the mountains."

Here was another ending.

The night before my early morning flight, Vince picked me up and drove me to Milan, where we shared a dinner with his partner, and I spent the night in his apartment, which was filled with intellectual artifacts, family photos, and old books. I contemplated every moment spent with my cousin, never finding an opportunity—which was in part, a consequence of his calculated ways of dodging the sentimental confrontation that I was trying to create—to articulate what his support meant to me. This was going to be harder than I thought. It is said that people's lives flash before their eyes as they transition from life to death, but there are so many micro-deaths and micro-births that occur within a life, the end of something and the start of another. I was beginning to mourn the loss of life as I knew it, of which Italy played a huge supporting role in keeping me sane and optimistic. These were my last hours in my mother's homeland, the country that I admired and longed to be a part of in more ways than just through visits and claimed roots. The reality of my decisions and choices was now starting to sink in. I was easily distracted with the excitement of starting life with the man I was in love with, but in the moments of solitude that I felt in my aunt's house late at night when everyone was in bed, or with Vince as we quietly strolled down the streets of Milan eating gelato, I reflected on the discernible ending of my wistful childhood.

I spent my last night in Italy sleepless. On the sleeper-sofa of Vince's apartment living room, I ruminated.

I was heartened by the thought that I didn't have a best friend to leave behind because both my best friends were already out of the country. Reem, with her family's support, had set her sights on Europe after her American education, and Cybèle, whom I stayed in touch with over the years through cards, letters, phone calls, and visits in Orlando during the 1990s, was in Canada since leaving Saudi in 1989.

I was grief-stricken about leaving Valentino behind.

By now I had lost both my Nonni. My Nonna lived a long and happy life and left us a few years earlier as she approached her 90s and after I had the chance to visit her several times as an adult. I tried not to think about my Zia. I knew she was dying, and I had to protect myself from mourning the event prematurely.

I tried to justify the impact of my decision on my father and my brother. I had put them in an onerous position. No one in our community had done what I was about to pull off. At moments I was angry that their desire to conform and please society was greater than their wish for my happiness.

I was hurt that my childhood hero, my father, never fought for me; he was the kindest man I knew but frustratingly reserved, absent. I was doleful that my image of him was altered as I grew to witness his broken spirit and fragile heart. The more I wanted to know him, the thicker his outer shell grew. He loved unconditionally, but that love was so implicit.

I reflected on my resentment toward my brother Yasser, who had so much authority over me, but who was also an anchor in our family and often rationalized societal absurdities for the sake of our survival. I had to trust that his astuteness would foster an eventual reconciliation, maybe even allowing us to have a stronger relationship than we ever could have imagined.

I was distraught about leaving behind my sister, May. When I left, we were not on very good terms. The tension in my life, of which she knew nothing, interfered with our ability to relate, and her life choices were weighing heavily on her, as she often strived to please everyone. This all culminated with a blow-up just weeks before I left. While I was relieved to hold her at a distance, I felt guilty about not saying goodbye. I knew ours was a temporary severance because we were too close to be permanently separated. I regretted, maybe selfishly, not telling her that I was finally stepping into the matrix of my fantasy.

I looked out the window in Vince's apartment living room at the bright August moon. I began to fight back tears.

Mamma. I felt like howling at the thought of not having her close. I wasn't sure how I was going to refuel without her influential pep talks and positive-thinking monologs. I had stored her teachings in my memory bank, and I knew I had them to fall back on, but hearing her voice and feeling her love was going to be something I knew would be painfully absent. I had a sudden inkling that these feelings were perhaps felt by her three decades ago, when she too left everything and everyone behind to follow her Arabian man and travel to a mysterious land. Unlike her I didn't know if or when I would ever see my family again. I had sacrificed my love for them and my dependence on them to gain personal freedom.

Inconceivably, I was going to America, with an American man, starting an American life, with a little blond American child. *What identity was I to assume? How do immigrants—without a family to keep them grounded in their origins and heritage—find a sense of belonging when taking the journey solo?*

I fretted about how I had never quite fit in Saudi Arabia or Italy. America, the cultural melting pot, united people in their American experience. Yet, I was intimidated by my lack of American cultural knowledge, beyond movies and TV. I didn't know what it was like to go to an American high-school or college. I wasn't sure if my diet would be corrupted with packaged goods and processed foods. I wondered if my sense of style would be modified. My mom admonished me before I left: "When you are finally in America, please don't leave the house in PJs and no eyeliner, make sure you fix yourself up when you're in public!"

Still wide awake, it was my last night in Italy, I got out of bed to repack my bag. I realized I wouldn't need my abaya handy for the trip. It was time to live without the shadow of religion following me everywhere, without the familiar nudge of guilt and judgment at every choice I made privately and publicly. I had so many questions about autonomy. *Would I understand all the cultural references and political jargon?* At twenty-five years of age, I would experience life as a newborn. I had the basics down, I could walk, talk, and wash/dress myself, but so many new daily habits and automatic reflexes were going to have to be learned in a blink of an eye if I were to stay afloat. I had to learn how to drive, how to advocate for myself, and how to interact with society as a person of value, as a woman.

Hours away, I was stepping on an airplane that was about to take me away. I had dreamed of America for so long, but it was only an illusion, until that moment. I had been a traveler my whole life, a good traveler, one who accepted the challenge of walking into the unexplored with the determination of an explorer, eager and ready to discover new things. Although my confidence had carried me this far, it was infused with my morbid fear of loss and plagued with insecurity. I could not have known that true courage manifested in moments of dire need, like now. I wish I could have comforted that young girl who feared losing her mother, her father, and herself, and assured her that she always wore the ruby slippers that gave her the power to be right where she belonged; and just like the Cowardly Lion in *The Wizard of Oz*, I was always the *king* of my own mental jungle. I was completely unaware that my desire for Darryl was the fuse that activated the courage to claim the life that I had been denied. *Did I know Darryl? Did I know what awaited me in Wyoming?* I was leaving all the familiar things behind: my parents, my siblings, even Valentino. I was heartbroken at the thought that some of the most comforting aspects of my life thus far, were out of reach during the most unpredictable journey of my life. And yet, no part of me second-guessed what I was doing.

At the Malpensa airport the next morning I was once again overtaken by unsettling worry. Darryl was to meet me before our flight to New York, *but what if he wouldn't show up? What if they held him in Riyadh? What if he changed his mind?*

This was it. The moment that would drastically alter the course of my life. My palms were sweaty, and my mouth was dry. I hoped Darryl would spot me from afar in my black jeans and white top. I was dressed in the most subdued way, hoping to blend in. My hair freshly trimmed into a neat bob after deciding to grow out my pixie cut. I knew Vince was talking to me, but I could not hear the sound of his voice over the sound of my pulse from my racing heart. I couldn't stop wondering about Darryl. Was he speculating what leaving his young child behind would feel like? Was he going to question whether leaving with me, for me, was worth it? I didn't grow up with the ability to have conversations about my personal feelings; I didn't know how to engage with Darryl about these floating doubts. If we had started our relationship as client and therapist where I merely shared some of my concerns in brief and swift sessions over a year ago, we were now placed in a far more vulnerable relationship where we would each have to open up and share our deepest fears, worries, hopes and dreams. Over the course of our short courtship, I saw no sign of him wanting to address these big questions, no invitation to speak about it, and no prompt to share anything. Perhaps this was how Western relationships were built? No talk of the past, just moving on. Perhaps it was temporary, and the future would be different.

My thoughts were interrupted when Vince exclaimed, pointing with a grin—"I think he's there!"—at a handsome brown-gray-bearded-clearly-not-Italian man in a navy-blue suit, speed walking toward me with a million-dollar smile. I dove into his embrace, smelling him, holding him, and almost fainting from the intoxicating feeling of having him so close to me again after several weeks apart. We stared at each other for a few seconds, unable to take a deep breath. I finally turned around and introduced Darryl to Vince.

I hugged my cousin tightly, and kissed him on the cheek, unable to express in words how grateful I was for his help, "Grazie, carissimo, arrivederci," was all I could say, as I kissed him one last time. He smiled with his eyes and blew me a kiss as the distance grew between us, "Ciao!" he finally said, softly.

When we walked away, Darryl asked me, "Can you believe this?" kissing my forehead.

I sighed. I was at a loss for words. My throat hurt from the lump that held back my tears of joy and sadness.

Darryl and I clasped hands tightly, and walked towards a café, my head pressing into his left side and our backpacks hanging on our opposite shoulders. My life had been a timebomb that now detonated—against all my apprehensions—*triumphantly*. The explosion was sweet. It was tender. It smelled like cappuccino.

At long last, this was it, my freedom.

EPILOGUE: A LETTER TO THE READER

"The great courageous act that we must all do, is to have the courage to step out of our history and past so that we can live our dreams."

—Oprah Winfrey

Dear Reader,

You have journeyed with me to the end of the book. I am grateful for your company. So much has changed in my life since that day at the airport in Milan with Darryl. It seemed appropriate to write an epilogue where I can briefly update you and share the mini sequel, *my life in America and the purpose behind writing this book.*

My story, while uncommon, is not unique in its struggle and determination. We have all longed for something that seemed so unattainable. Over the years I have met so many people who shared their intimate challenges and who showed me we are all one; all of us seek love and acceptance and the dignity to live our lives as authentically as possible. Freedom seemed like a worthy goal, a priceless reward for the sacrifices that life challenged me with. When I left, I never looked back, but I knew I had to come to terms with my identity and my truth. At the time, I had hoped that I would one day be able to acknowledge the wonderful traits and historic contributions of my people, but I was not ready to disclose all the painful and embarrassing failings of my cultural upbringing, not even anticipating the horror and shame that was to multiply after 9/11, which only put me at odds with my focused attempt to assert a neutral selfhood after my arrival in America; an attempt, that you can imagine, triggered a new trauma, magnifying the terror of the past I had escaped. It took twenty years, but today, I have come to terms with all of it, I am proud and grateful for all the pieces that make me whole. *That is why I wrote this book.*

Starting a family was the remedy I needed to heal from that past; we built a solid foundation for a future that I knew would not be free of pain and drama. Darryl and I started our journey in the peaceful and quiet state of Wyoming, a perfect place to wholesomely nest. We parented Zachary six months of the year, and in the first three years, I chose to bond with him tightly before we welcomed another child into our family. Dante was born a year after 9/11, a pregnancy that was marked by so many grand changes in me and the world. A couple of years after that, our youngest, Eros, helped me fulfill a maternal desire to give birth at home, with his daddy and brothers by our side. Our family was complete, with a lovely cozy home, a green yard, and a golden lab, named Baca. We homeschooled our children and traveled all over the United States in our motorhome and camping gear; I got to see the country I finally felt I belonged to, north to south, and east to west. We managed to raise a happy and healthy family, and there were times when I knew I had hit the jackpot. There were also dark days when I feared we would never be free of Darryl's old wounds and the trauma that tormented him, which he tried hard to bury and conceal.

Ours was a love story that only blooms once in a lifetime, and with all the theatrics that accompany a story like ours, there was comedy, poetry, music, adventure, and tragedy. When Darryl chose to become a therapist, he did so because he said he understood the pain of his patients. He empathized with their turmoil and related to their mental illness. I knew his grief, stemming from childhood secrets and generational strife, had haunted him his whole life. I had wished to see him triumph over his demons, but we cannot change the course of someone's destiny without their will to do so. After ten years spent together living passionately, both in bliss and agony, we ended our marriage. My love for Darryl was replaced with my commitment to our children and their right to have a life free of agitation and instability. Darryl's journey was a difficult one to witness, and it excruciates me to share that following the loss of his mother and a battle fought privately with prescription pill addiction, Darryl took his own life. What remains from our touching and daring love story is the most beautiful and powerful symbols any two lovers can create: Three sons who have brought me the greatest joy. I see the better, braver, and brighter versions of me and Darryl in them every day. I thought freedom was the worthiest cause for any sacrifice, until the day I became a mother and realized that Zac, Dante, and Eros are the reasons for my very existence, and that I have been bestowed with the privilege of a lifetime as their mother.

Becoming an American also meant embracing the magic and accepting the horrors of my new country. America remains a beacon of hope for many, foremost me, and I celebrate the resilience of its people when she gravely disappoints them through unamended laws and lop-sided privileges. I could never compare the challenges of my early life with the challenges of marginalized Americans. The experiences exist in different dimensions, but the struggle of the oppressed is one. *That is why I wrote this book.*

As a third culture child I always searched for answers in justice advocates and compassionate leaders. Dr. Martin Luther King Jr., a Baptist minister from Georgia, somehow landed on my radar when I was a teen. In movies and documentaries, I saw him speak to his people and for his people, in a country that he believed made him a promise to exist with dignity and respect. He brought to light the atrocities of a history that no one wanted to confront. His message was heard around the world. And while his lens focused on the racial injustices of Black Americans, his plea for freedom and virtue resonated with all oppressed peoples. I heard him, I reacted to his message, I wished the whole world could hear it. But if his urgent message continues to be the cry of American generations long after his death, how could I expect that the rest of the world is paying attention to the human rights violations in my land of birth? This sentiment multiplied within my very core, when in 2018, while my father took his very last breath far away from me, Saudi journalist Jamal Khashoggi was brutally murdered by a system, that decades after my departure, remains corrupt, unjust, untouched, and atrocious. Because we are now a global community, we can no longer pretend that what happens in one part of the world does not concern us. As a child I felt abandoned by the rest of the world because my existence resembled that of the creatures in Whoville, a place not many knew existed or cared about even when told. There are children, women, and even men in places around the world who feel abandoned and forgotten. They will not be as lucky as me. *That is why I wrote this book.* "We've GOT to make noises in greater amounts! So open your mouth, lad! For every voice counts!" (Dr. Seuss, 1954).

Some might believe only fearless people can make changes and become part of the shift that is needed in the world. What is courage if there is no fear? Nelson Mandela famously said, "Courage is not the absence of fear, but the triumph over it. The brave man is not he who does not feel afraid, but he who conquers that fear."

Looking back, I know my courage as a child is the only reason I am here today. On that fateful evening when I was six years old, lying on the ground, peeking through the bottom of the main gate of our yard, waiting for my mom to return from a visit to a friend, I felt fear and anxiety at the thought of her not coming home. This was the event that sparked my awareness that life is unpredictable and uncertain. I was too young to have to live with that unfair degree of worry and fear, but I have no qualms about the fact that it was the instant in which I learned to face the one thing I am most afraid of, loss. I could have stayed in my room crying or distracted myself with my toys. Instead, I chose to spend the hours that my mom was gone facing that fear head on, anticipating the possible reassurance that she would come back. My tenacity was always rewarded, and that established a sense of trust that my fears are not greater than my resilience. With that same attitude I faced my new life away from everything I had ever known. I survived the intense haboob and plunged into the abyss of a deeply unidentified future.

Today I live in the Pacific Northwest, where I share my dreams and hopes with a progressive, like-minded community, and with Thom, my thoughtful, loving husband who embodies the balance between dreaming big and remaining grounded. He is my anchor and my strongest supporter. I am in love in a very different and gratifyingly, evolving way. I see nothing but trees when I look out the windows of my home, and from my doorstep I can walk to the South Puget Sound beaches of the Evergreen State. I have always had a dog by my side, sometimes two at a time, and never take for granted the gift of cuddling my sweet, departed Kiki, or taking Gaia on walks and hikes. I love gardening and feel close to my Nonno and Zia when I pick my green beans and zucchini. I found home in Buddhism, yoga, and meditation and appreciate a hot cup of fair-trade organic coffee, an homage to my Italian blood and adopted Northwest lifestyle. I watch my sons facing their adulthoods, questioning the meaning of life and their purpose, all while exploding without constraints in their talents and passions, from music, to engineering, and everything in between. I see Darryl in their pensive eyes and hear him in their hearty laughs.

A brush with the impermanence of life pushed me to actively manifest the next chapter in my story; after spending years fearing, worrying, and stressing, the child in me finally said goodbye to Nebras as she bravely appeared one last time to give me strength. I was diagnosed with breast cancer in my early 40s and that encounter was perhaps, thus far, the greatest guru of all. It propelled me to live fiercely and calmly, ultimately interlocking my yin and yang to find physical, mental, and emotional balance. I fulfilled my educational goals and celebrated my father's impressive academic journey when I pursued my graduate degree. I specialized in ethical leadership and social equity. Using my story and my education, I speak and lecture on cross-cultural issues, I host a podcast, and teach, all in the hope to raise awareness and understanding of my culture, on identity, and on the imperativeness of gender equality, ethical equity, and social justice.

I am also happy to share that I remained in touch with the marvelous Ms. Boissel; I continue to share a close and rich friendship with Reem; and Cybèle, now an honorary auntie to my sons, works for an airline company and visits us multiple times a year from Canada. As for my dear cousin Vince, I can proudly say that he and I share a reverence for our ancestral tree; we remain very close and have become the thread that holds our family's fabric across time and continents.

It is true that life can be stranger than fiction; my nuclear family's update is one that I could not have conjured up even if I had tried. During my first three years in America, I had no contact with my father and brother. It was painful to feel so disposable, but I knew it was their pain, along with their pride, that held them hostage. After my son Dante was born, I wrote a letter to my father—with photos—and informed him that his first grandchild had been born and that he had a bonus grandchild named Zachary. Children offer many miracles, their sheer existence is a gift we cannot fully comprehend, but my children tore down the wall of hurt that stood between me and my father. I never saw my Papà after leaving Saudi Arabia in 1999, but we spoke on the phone and video chat often, and his room was a shrine to his American grandchildren. During my last conversation with him, he told me he was proud of me, perhaps it was a subconscious notion of his nearing end, but it was uncharacteristic of him to speak so intimately. I told him I wanted to write a book about my life, about my family. His pride and trust in me had finally set him free and he gave me his blessings, "Brava, you are a writer like your Mamma." He said as his chuckled jauntily.

After spending the last fifteen years between her time in Wyoming and Washington with grandsons and her life in Saudi Arabia, my Mamma permanently moved to the United States post-retirement, and now lives with me and my family, where her presence enriches our lives with warmth, wisdom, and unconditional love. My sister May and my brother Yasser also immigrated to the United States a decade after me. It seems impossible that after feeling betrayed and hurt due to my bold escape, they have not only reconciled with my choices, but rekindled our kinship in more rewarding ways than I thought possible. With deep gratitude, I marvel at our bonds, but mostly at how they have been able to give themselves permission to pursue their happiness; they obtained their freedom deliberately, without the terror and heartbreak I couldn't avoid.

If I had proceeded with anything less than the audacity to concoct a pipe dream, my life would have inevitably taken a very different turn. With every bump in the road, I felt forced to press on. I deserted all familiar measures and accomplished the ultimate promise to myself. I embarked on the impossible journey, with the spirit of a renegade because I believed in the unbelievable dream. I succeeded because I was selfish in chasing the life I knew I deserved.

"*Without leaps of imagination, or dreaming, we lose the excitement of possibilities. Dreaming, after all, is a form of planning.*"

—*Gloria Steinem*

I wanted the opportunity to make a difference in my life and, consequently, in the lives of others. I trusted that I could raise my children openly without the physical and intellectual threats I endured. I was set on one day walking a happy tail-wagging puppy to the park on a real leash.

I made it. I am here because of the people, who along my journey, opened my eyes, my mind, and my heart. I am here because of my lack of preconceived expectations, and the unrepentant determination to seize my destiny, my freedom.

With love,
Jasmin